Kevs

WAKE

UP

Australia

ISBN: 978-0-6452499-7-2

Kev's- WAKE-UP - Australia-

IS-- The Story of- How--

The "Elders" Created--

The Greatest Australia Day

"Furphy"

The WORLD--Has EVER Seen-

A- 185+ Year Old- "Furphy"--

Alive & Well--TODAY.!

AS--There was--

NO Waterloo Creek *Massacre*--

It's an Elders-BIG "Furphy".?

And there IS More.

By- aussiekevG.

ISBN: 978-0-6452499-7-2

Kev's- WAKE-UP- Australia-

WAKE-UP Australia-
we ALL *Should*--
   Celebrate **Australia Day**--
we ALL *Should*--
   Celebrate **Darwin War** Day.

the power of *truth-telling*--reveals--

The Greatest "Furphy"-- EVER Seen.!

Fully Endorsed-- BY — aussiekevG.

Publishers:-- "aussiekevG."
Copyright:--"aussiekevG."

The Right of "aussiekevG" to be identified as the author of this work has been asserted by him under Copyright Amendment (Moral Rights) Act 2000.
ISBN Cataloguing No: 978-0-6452499-7-2
Please Note: --
This Book IS <u>Meant</u> to be Un-ashamedly- "Different" --
Because The **Author**-- 'aussiekevG.'--IS--"Different".!

This Book is Copyright — The Material and its Presentation has been created and edited for print by 'Kev': material is Not Typeset. Kev is Not A 'Trained' Writer-- The Material was drawn from Own Computer'-
Kev writes as/is- copy to Print for Personal Presentation herein.
Kev does Not advise On Human Relations nor Investments--IS Not-- herein suggesting anything outside the Proper Uses for any of aussiekevG's/KPG.**Products.**

Those seeking Human Relations or Investment advice--should consult-- <u>Un-biased</u> Registered Advisors.
This work Can Not be used in part, or total, by any means without prior-- written permission by aussiekevG/KPG. esq.

Attached: IN Word: Book Antiqua 10- 12 -16.Pt.
    Cover Design: by The Author.
    Printed & Bound by 'aussiekevG'. esq.
    We Promote Sustainable Forests etc.

<u>AUTHOR</u>: -- aussiekevG.
    Australia-
For Further Details--
.   **Contact Kev by Email at:** authorkevg@bigpond.com

I Need- To Thank People

First-- to Thank my wife- who has Helped with her patience and understanding of 'A Writer' who doesn't work 'Regular' Hours and writes such material as herein. I Also wish To Thank all **'The Subject Writers'- and 'Image' producers-** and to clarify that-- there Are NO Original Blacks or Whites Alive-and So- I have written My Story--within and around material images- trying not to Alter Intent-- but to show How Records and Reports can and do vary- In hope-I can convey 'My Message' and do so in a way that—in a sense- we seem to work 'Together'- to Help **avoid-** what I CAN See as—

A Racial Disaster surely looming- which My Research says- IS Based on mostly-- "Un-Proven"-- "Made-Up"--Facts.!
I Thank those of whose material I have used herein to tell this Story and- IF I have not mentioned any-by Name- then I am sorry-but if you would Contact me at- authorkevg@bigpond.com with Heading 'Correction'--
I can try to amend that asap. I Do Thank Encyclopaedia Britannica- for Images- notes etc. used—Also as--I Started my Sales Career with EB - before Computers and I Learnt of "Brainwashing" Techniques and Sold many EB's to People in all walks of life--In 'The Days'- long before The Internet. I Thank Google- Wikipedia- Wikimedia- Tas Govt. Etc. The York Gate Library-South Australia–for their material—

I also Thank—'Dizzy'-as it was his Comments- in Herald Sun-- Nov. 13/2021- As:--
"*I just wish people would listen and learn*"- as got me going- that some "parody". But- I admired ' Dizzy' for his Cricket Exploits for Australia-- And--Now-I try to Show Him--and ALL Australia - that They should "*Study MY Theme* and- Learn to live--
A United-- Harmonious Future- "Together".!
I Am NOT 'Anti- Aboriginal'-- It's that My Un-Bias Research has shown mostly The 'Real Truths' -that are Not being used by Aboriginal writers who are so Bias and don't concede-- that none Can ever know exactly what happened and/or why--and I say WE Do ALL need to CHANGE Our Thinking--IF we are to ever work together- To take advantage of what has been Built-and created- To Enjoy **The Incredible** Future Opportunities—"Together.!
Check "Kev's Books List " on Page 297 herein.

aussiekevG.

Kev's- WAKE UP- Australia-
Using—'Aboriginal' Web Sites "Theme"--

'the power of *truth-telling* to realise change'
This 'Action Line'—Helped me--
"Re- Wright History"--

The Aboriginal Story IS about--
'Confusion' -'Contradiction'- 'Collusion'-
and much more--

IS Why- I Present My Story--

To First--SAY-- TO All--

"ITS TIME"--

ITS TIME-- To Change Direction--

ITS TIME-- To "WAKE UP"--

Because--I 'SEE'--

A Racist Disaster Looming.?

Table Of Contents

Prologue	Page-10-
Introduction-	P-17-
SUMS say We Should be EVEN--	**P-30-**
SORRY-	P-34-
Return To Our Culture--	P-41-
WHAT IF--Hypothetically—	P-52-
The Author Background--	**P-76-**
History	P-88-
The Power of Dream-time Stories	P-107-
The 1942 Darwin War	**P-116-**
The Landing	P-131-
Other Opinions--	P-139-
"Fabrication Of Massacres"	P-150-
Misconceptions	P-162-
A Voice--	P-181-
Waterloo Creek Massacre **"Furphy"**	P-197-
OUR History-	P-224-
Change The Date-- WHY.?	P-232-
Australian Pre-History-	P-240-
Who Was Here First-	
Weapons & WARS-	P-265-
We Should Be **EQUAL-**	P-290
SUMMARY-	P- 291-
Author Kev's- Book List-	P-299-
TO ORDER Kev's Books-	
Kev's *'Mind Train'* CARDS--	P-302-

Prologue

This Book-- IS about "the Aboriginal story" —

Written by *aussiekevG*. --<u>a proud Australian</u> with Family History from 1878- where My Ancestors- ran The First coach service from Lorne Victoria. But Here-

When relating to 'The Claims' of *Hundreds of Thousands of OUR Ancestors were Slaughtered or Massacred by The British--*

My Logic --answers that- **with ONE question-** <u>as</u> <u>like</u>:--

IF- so many <u>Thousands</u> of Your Ancestors were Killed- as each Do Claim — THEN- How did You all- Come to BE Here.? Where did You come from- as Your Ancestors were all Killed.?   <u>Simple Question</u>-? Likely-- <u>Simple Answer</u>- Right.?

FIRST To Note —

This material is written with due respects as I/Kev- am- an untrained Writer- who writes- as I See IT- and some will Agree some will Disagree with My Comments — which I do expect. Here- I write because IN 'Today's'- totally unchecked- One-Sided Situation —

SOMEONE Needs To SAY Something.!

I Point out YES — This Book was ready to go to Publishers — before The Vote for "The Voice" — I withheld IT — Because--

I Did NOT want My Book to 'Influence' people who were going to Vote — One way or The Other.!

Albeit — I did not believe The Referendum would Win-- Not-- because IT may not be good for Indigenous People — but — because to me- it simply was A Politicians EGO TRIP and most times they are never Good for anyone — least of all for-- Those who are proposed/or supposed- to be 'Helped'-- by it. Here it was our PM-- where The Irony always would be that A Political Group can't be sure They <u>will be</u> *In Power* beyond The Next Election- when- with due respects- They could well then be "In Opposition" — and Can't DO what was promised.!
BUT-- As I explain herein--I See 'The Problem' IS that 'The Aboriginals' Do truly believe *'They are Owed'*-

I explain Why--as I point out- having perused The Aboriginal Web Sites-- Read so much Material- where- try as I did — I could Not Find ONE Site who even included more that 1- 2 Lines as related to *"The Darwin War".?* Nor any referring to *"The Significance"* of this War **for The Future of** the whole Aboriginal Race.!
NOW — as I read many Reports- most included by Aboriginal "Activists"- I found *"Creative Things"*- A Web Site- set up by *"A well- meaning"* Non-aboriginal man whose Aim is stated as to *"Help Me Understand Aboriginal History"*-- and it says that-- *'Here--I can obtain material for A Project'* etc. But on further perusal--I did find that This Site too--features Articles as are also written mainly By Aboriginals- and as such-- I again am reading Totally Bias Stories- which- In My Opinion do nothing more than Help Divide Our Australian Population- and Teach this man nothing — because here- as in other 'Aboriginal Web- Sites' they are still intent on "Looking Back" trying to Prove Thousands of their Ancestors were massacred. Again recently- I read of- listened to 'Aunty Glenda Chalker' - who also-- spoke of *'Other ways to Share/change Australia Day- Date'- where* She too- I See--is still focused on "Looking Back"- at everything about **The 1788 "Invasion"** and **The Massacre at Waterloo Creek in 1838 –** where they say- Hundreds/even 1,000's were slaughtered "by Soldiers of The First Fleet"-- But then- in The Old Newspaper Reports as were shown on the Sites. Again- they only refer to/feature 'Things' as done TO Blacks-- Few relate to atrocities ON Whites-- eg:--I read where *'One White man was killed – and his Hands were cut Off —* here- The Aboriginal Killer- sought to have some Food-Put in The open Palm of The Hand--IN return- for pulling 'Sinew's' to make The Fingers work--as a Joke situation. BUT--*This was* NOT an atrocity- and mention of *'Killing The White and Cutting Off His Hands'* etc-- was covered in just 2-3 Lines.!

Whereas--The Aboriginal *"Factual"* Report of "The Appin Massacre" as example-- was covered in so much confusing-misleading Detail—featuring 'Soldiers' who were not there- where even Books of 'Made-Up' Facts-- are written on The Subject—

Yes- **Everywhere I Look** – each Aboriginal HAS become-- *"An Activist"* and Total attention IS on The 1788 Invasion and The Loss of Their Ancestors- Their Land and Their Customs—

IN most cases Spoken by some well- Educated Aboriginals who have Gained such Education—<u>Because</u> The First Fleet Did Come to this Country—yet they still seem committed on gaining some Benefits or Treaty or other- as result of this Claim--that Thousands of Their Ancestors were massacred by the First Fleet Invaders.

I truly have **Not Read so much ONE- Sided Logic in all of my Life.** To me--
IT seems All the "Activists"-each have like--
A Ruled OFF Page- and anything other than How badly Their Ancestors were Treated or Slaughtered--by The Thousands-- just has NO Place on That Page.
And somehow—They never seem to 'Logic' that IF so many Thousands of "Their" Ancestors WERE—Slaughtered—How then was it possible that 'They' ARE Here now--Today.?
Where did 'They' come from.?

SO YES—
SOMEONE from the 96.7%-- Needs To SAY Something.!

SO Then--**To decide to Write this Book** the first question I had to ask Myself was--Why would I decide to write a book about 'Aboriginals' when there are- already a 100+ Totally **Bias** Books written on the subject.?
Short answer is-because Revered historical writers- 'Experts' aunts- uncles- ABC presenters- *'super educated'* University professors- pretend 'senators'- historical experts as 'Renee' works with- LinkedIn 'friends'- Academics- Ex Sports Champs and Dizzie (his H/sun post- grabbed me) All who suddenly 'Find' Allegiance and bias to Aboriginals and write their 'FACTS' on *Colonisation* **'Wars'-and** **'Genocide'**- even to have someone with direct Links to 'Massacres' etc-
Well although- I did NOT have their Top Education-- *(I left school at 14)* **But-- I am** actually **writing this story--** *"to help them"* --To help them- One and all- because they just don't seem to understand- How- totally *'singular'* their attitudes are toward the 3.3% Aboriginals- with their One *eyed look'* at a subject they know *'Little'* about--which is why they all seem to have *"same problems"*- like a *'One eyed view'*- *'One dimensional type memory'*- and- their Wont- to accept "Elders" *made up stories*- as Passed on- at face value- and as the historical writers wrote **their 'Facts'**- 200 years later- using *'Sensationalism'* To Sell their books or videos- movies etc-- to make money for them. ***None of which DID Help The Aboriginals — or did help stop Their Racism.!***
NOW — I am Not saying One should Not Read their Books — but I say- Do as I do- grab A Notepad- and as you Read-- make A Note down Left side-number of Native/Aboriginals The Writer says were Slaughtered--Massacred etc- then Down Right side — Note Number of Bodies or Body Bones a writer 'Found' within their claims- then at bottom of the Pad Tally them Up --Make Your Own decision as to credibility of These Writers — Yes Of course I do know- The Answer.!

But as I Prove herein—IT Is NOT that the other 96.7% of Australians don't Accept that many "Things" did happen during Colonisation—But-- they see- it was Blacks and Whites and these People get that-- It Is NOT Possible to know what happened or why and that-- WE—*The People of Today*—Are NOT Responsible— Nor can we Change what happened in The Past—

SAME as the 3.3% Aboriginals CAN'T Deny that IF ever they were Owed any "DEBT"- as result of their Colonisation Claims as eg:- *They Slaughtered Our Kin--Stole Our Land-Took* away *Our Culture--*SURELY- ANY Such Debt-- HAS Been **Long "Paid"-** and PAID In FULL- Plus some.!

Because:--

IF The British--The 96.7% of Aussie Population--
    Had NOT been here-- *in 1942* —

TO re-iterate --

*IF They were NOT Here--*The Japanese Army Invasion-- Would have <u>*Wiped Out*</u> **The Whole Aboriginal Race.**
IF-- That had happened- then:--
How could these So-well Educated Aboriginals have gained their Education- How could they have gained Opportunities for Growth and Assets—How could They have Grown in-- Sport or Business as So many are involved IN here Today.?
THE REALITY IS — <u>*IF the 96.7%-- were NOT There--*</u>

HOW Could The Aboriginals have been Here Today.?

Because- It WAS The British who Did REPEL The Japanese Army Invasion *at* Darwin *in 1942-and IF They had NOT Been Here-* The Japanese Army *would have* Massacred the whole Aboriginal Race-!
SO- All of The Long-standing est. Debt **with All** The Claims SHOULD Have Died right there — IN Darwin **in 1942.!**

There should have been **NO Protests** and **NO False Claims.!**
From then on to today as ALL Should have agreed NOW-- WE are EVEN.!
Then came "The Voice" — where eventually after A Strident 'YES' Campaign — Led surprisingly By Our Prime Minister-- **IT Was defeated by 61% who Voted NO-- to installing 'The Voice' on behalf All Aboriginals — IN Our Constitution--** Here I see — such a large number who Voted NO — did not Vote NO because they don't want to Accept or want to Help The Aboriginals — NO. I See- It was because they want the 3.3% of Aboriginals to relate to 'Things'- like--
How VERY Important the 'Darwin War' Was To Aboriginals and that The Aboriginals ONE and ALL — Should NOT Forget This WAR — Because IT was NOT Just **"Life Saving"** — IT was SAVING -The Whole Aboriginal RACE — AND--
The Darwin War **SAVED** The Whole Aboriginal Race
I See-- The NO Voters- really were Saying —
That--Once The Aboriginals- Do accept that Reality- which Is ALL True--completely Factual- and Its ALL-- On Record.!

Then we can "Accept each other" as being EQUAL--
and then We can-LOOK Forward- and 'Move On' Together We Can begin to share and enjoy--what Has been Built — for ALL to enjoy.!
I Have Done The SUMS and My Chart on Page 30 Shows —
WHY — I Say ANY Such Debt — WAS Fully Paid in 1942 — when The Japanese Army- attempted to INVADE Australia and would have *Wiped Out--*The Aboriginal Race-
IF--The Other 96.7% of The Population were Not Here — AND All of My Research confirms--
　　　　THAT-- to be A PROVEN FACT.!
　　　　　Author- aussiekevG.

Introduction

SO--HERE--I write because-- its time **Someone** from the **96.7% of Our Australian Population-** *Said something*-- As we can't have- **'Our History'**- created by what these bias 'profiteers' wrote- when they say things focused on proving 'Massacres' that mostly **Only occurred** IN Their books- like one wrote *20,000 natives were slaughtered in colonisation*--yet there- as others- they have found NO Bodies nor Body bones-to support these claims-- Why.?
Obvious answer-to me = *there were NO bodies there- to find.!* No- ironically there is No Record of finding any of the 20,000 Bodies as they Claimed as being "Slaughtered"--Equally as - there is No Record of the *to 300 slaughtered* as R-Milliss Claims at Start of His Book--**Oh shock horror--NO Bodies--** nor Body Bones were found here either-**surprise-Surprise.?** No- because whatever they wrote or said- is *mostly* **their Own made-up Crap-** YES made-up Crap--some almost *criminal-* **in** what they wrote **of** what 'they' knew of Slaughter deaths in Colonisation of Australia.
When--"They" wrote mostly own made-up Rubbish-- and I wish the aboriginals of today--would stop- *'open the other eye'* and read what I write here- because the activists of today- **just don't get it — they won't accept--** that the Deadly things as *"frontier wars"* and *"genocide"* were not heard of-- Till the esteemed writers included them within their books or videos & Movies etc. To help them Sell their books/and their products-- **Not to help the Aboriginals-- by printing Facts.!**
Same as "The Elders' so **conveniently** didn't want to accept or understand that The British in 1788 came in peace- they did not bring Army or guns to- as "the -activists" say- *wipe out the natives--take away their culture-* NO--
FACT IS — That On Arrival- Captain Phillip-was appalled- when he found- after the 55,000 years of claimed occupation- there was No decent housing--No permanent food Supply-

No medical or hospital--No schools — No 'trade Training'-
No Defence etc-- and Ironically--the journals say- during
Capt. Phillips 4-year term there were few problems. Except
many of his convicts--Died from illness- some were killed by
natives- yet there were just 4 natives as died/or were killed--
Capt. Phillip became friends with *Pemulwuy* who supplied
'meat' on contract to the colony-when the supply ships were
late *arriving*. Then after 'a friendly' kidnap of Bennelong and
Colby- to try to convince them- *they could help each other* —
He to learn their language and customs- they to learn to
Read and Write 'English' and more which appeared to work-
As-- soon — A Friend of Bennelong- called Yemmerrawanne
also joined the Group.
My research found--problem has always been- aboriginals
are victims of 'a ***brainwashing***' continuous Technique as has
been used by "Elders"--Constantly from way back there-
and- "the activists" of today — make *no allowance for* the fact
that-- 'the British' have *done everything* that Captain Phillip
promised the natives ("their ancestors") that He would Do--
to Help them. He *the British*- built better Housing- grew
more varied- consistent Food supply- incl. breed cattle-
sheep etc. To install A Hospital- Medical/doctor care —
introduce Schools and Education systems- to Protect young
aboriginals from in-breeding and family abuse. They built a
Defence system — then fought with allied Countries to-
Declare Our independence — But to also gain "back-up" from
these 'Allies'--IF we were ever attacked.!
AS- Japan Did Attack--and DID "invade" Australia via
Darwin-- **in 1942** — when our Allies- Did come to our aid
and with their help Aussies and Aboriginals fought Together
and--**We Did win** the Darwin War — We did drive Japan
from our shores — We Did **SAVE Australia** — ALSO--

20

DID- SAVE the aboriginals. YES we won the Darwin war- creating **Unity — Friendship** and **Mateship-**
THESE are things as should "Feature" **IN "The History"** — Of **"Our Country".!**

I will talk of these 'things' herein — and also include a section on "weapons & wars" on page 261 as also to include A Copy of My "Balance sheet" on Page 31 which shows numbers claimed- of Aboriginals killed-as it presents the tally of lives- we lost in all of the wars which demonstrates Why *I say* — *Loudly that-* **We should be Even- we should start again** AS **we should Celebrate** "*Australia day*" as "*Darwin war day*" **Together- Unity** should be created for All to work together in Harmony- from here on--To accept there was-- **NO Massacre** at **waterloo creek** as — There was **NO Invasion** in 1788--But—

There was **a Real Invasion** in **Darwin in 1942** — *I say:-* **if--Our History is to be written — to present to young children at schools--**it should be aimed at highlighting— **This UNITY--** It should include how even as far back as 'the Boar' war- Gallipoli-etc. *Aboriginals* did fight with Aussies and Allies- in all the wars- right through to **the Japanese** Army attack on Darwin in 1942- where aboriginals did also fight with Aussies and Allies to drive Japan from Our Shores. This is the Direction **"Our History"** should be heading-- to Promote --Demonstrate- and Maintain-- **this "Unity".!** To highlight the feature of Australia being-- one *multi-cultural population* with multi- mindset and diversity all melding together to be adding their own piece- to this giant landscape. Where we have the reputation as being so progressive in our thinking and creativity with views for —

A Better future- Yet still today whilst 'activists' have become better educated —

Here these descendants are using their Great Education--
And 'Positions' to motivate the less educated- to rebel
against-- The British/The Government--using totally false
"true facts" as were passed on to them by their *'truth telling'*
elders-- always to present a One-dimensional attack—
continually still *trying to --Divide our nation.!* Planning on
dividing us more by-- teaching our children of "Aboriginal
made-up " History- which means it's **NOT--"Our History"**- It
is the aboriginal history — as written by these Sensationalist
writers with *"made-up stories"* — first as passed down by
"truth telling elders"--ALL likely- **False**- or *made-up* Stories
of "massacres" and "slaughters"- which were then
embellished- by The Writers- who wrote 'things' as likely
did Not happen- *Except* **IN Their Books--Videos--Movies
etc--**where None of the Thousands of bodies claimed as were
massacred- slaughtered-- **have ever been found**.?
These things-as aboriginals say- do represent Our History- I see--
will only divide the population further- than it already has--
Where I say:--**It's a crazy cycle--** because their titles even to
honours from the Queen (RIP)--then books and reports that
they have published, all have been helping to form *disregard
within the minds of the young aboriginal generations--*Who have-
Read the literature — listened to the lectures of/by these
"Experts" who do sound to talk as if--they really were there-
and so they Do know — IS Why Young Aboriginals Should
Believe Them — and They DO — Believe These "Stories".!
But of course- we know-- they were Not there- yet few if
any do as 'professor Ann McGrath' wrote- years ago- to say
that Her *Stories* are **"made up"** of *historic imagination and
narration--* put together to create a good story-- **NOT Facts.!**
SO- the problem we have today- as I can see- really began
'way back'- almost Two Centuries before movie maker--
Andrew Pike and aboriginal-wife Dr Merrilyn Fitzpatrick-

Coupled with professor Ann McGrath- decided they could tell The Story of the Aboriginals- or- Tell **"Their" Aboriginal** Story-- better in — Their movies-- Not true "factual" stories- but *"made-up stories*--Which actually do follow "the trend" set by the early "Elders"

And- was helping to subtly create False images and — to Give False impressions in the minds of the many thousands of our young aboriginals who sadly-- do most always **believe** that-- What they were seeing- hearing and or reading--Was True.! To produce a good story yes-**but** they were *'made up stories'* and ***not facts***.!

It is ironic that- the education gained by those who had used everything initially established by Capt. Phillip--as later helped gain their higher educations and respected positions- They now use this to be an "Activist" — instead of using it to help grow and maintain **Unity** — they choose to foster Their **Division** — As featured on aboriginal web sites where they build and create "Stories" to make any situations as reported in early 'Gazettes' look to mean how they-want it to read-by dissecting letters or changing words of governors- or only use "parts" of Reports which will- make "the British" invaders-- look as if they--had committed more "Massacres" such as the esteemed professor Ryan *"proves"* with her-- "massacre map".? I have perused much of this material- yet only "parts" of those reports as I found were used in aboriginal websites and Other "Stories"- like my great-great-great grandmother "Said"--and 'this story' is written as such was Said- "last week"-and it is presented- as A Fact.?

Like that's 5-6-even 7-8+ times that "Story" was 're-written' and re-passed on — each one also adding or deleting parts of the message — and yet today- 200+ years later- IT is being presented as "A Fact".? This is the type of things that I am writing about herein where 'activists' are mostly- sadly--

Sidestepping- avoiding the understanding and acceptance-- of how their whole lives, have been built upon "The elders"- *made-up* "stories" as they accepted as being True--when most were always just "*made-up Stories*"--**Not facts** or reports of any **"real events"**--but "*made-up*" Stories-Aimed at creating a mindset to believe *"the invaders"* HAD--Slaughtered or Massacred many thousands of their ancestors.! **Yet in hindsight** there were NO Bodies ever found- anywhere-to support their claims — Other than those few On-Record.!

Yet the younger aboriginals did not ask *why this was so*- nor did They ask *"what happened to all of the bodies.?* Yes--over and over again these "messages" have been "fed" into their minds-- continually by their trusted "*truth telling*--Elders"-- Cleverly changed- altered 5-6 times- then *made-up*- or with things added-- Constantly passing them on- and-- feeding them to their Kin-as True. Just so many *false made-up reports*- Of the "slaughters or **massacres**"- as likely did NOT ever happen- as the 'stories'--were un-truths or made-up facts-- Such as *Elders said*--1,000's massacred at waterloo creek — IS Why we need to Change The Date of Our Australia Day.! But yet-- just 7- yes ***Seven*** *were Killed* — *10-12 were also Shot* — *but just 7 Were Killed* — The Bodies were returned to The Colony as 'Retribution' for The Ones who earlier had Killed the Un-Armed Settlers and these 7 Bodies **ARE--On Record.** This deceit/distortion of truths- to me seems likely to have-- begun- way back- when "the leading elders from "the gulf"-- Sent messages to **tell all that:--**
"*Pemulwuy's wife & un-born child*" ***were killed*** *by The British Invaders* **w***hich was when--Pemulwuy turned against Captain Phillip and led his fight to force the British from their land.!*
When- in fact — The journals had earlier said that This man-- Pemulwuy had been--a friend to Capt. Phillip- his wife was ready to have her baby — so Captain Phillip —

Had offered use of hospital as help of doctor and nurse to his friend- alas the Wife wanted to give birth with her elders. Pemulwuy then convinced her to go to the hospital--on Phillip's urging- but- when 'complications' set in at birth-- she refused doctors help-and got worse, till she and the baby sadly--both died.!

It appears "the lead Elders" of "the gulf of Carpentaria" area Then used this **"Killing"** (died in childbirth)- in their -- 'Dreaming stories' — saying this was the reason why they did not try to come talk to Capt. Phillip-try to bridge a Language gap. It gave them an excuse- to amplify the desire to Force the invaders-**'the killers'**- from their land--Not to Share with them.

To motivate other tribes to fight--**drive** the British **"killers"**-- From our land — disregarding the things as Capt. Phillip had- Started to help them with- most importantly-build a Defence Because he had told them--*they were prone to attack from non-friendly Nations — and also-they should enjoy--the 'things' as would be built here — for all people to share.* BUT Yes- motivated by those "Elders"--'Pemulwuy' blamed Capt. Phillip for his loss- which was when he began His **constant guerrilla type** destructive fighting and resistance-against the settlers--**in revenge.** He created a gang- they burnt crops, burnt houses- stole food- killed stock--Capt. Phillip had 'tolerated' this - because he knew it was against Him- till then Pemulwuy began to kill 'un-armed' settlers- so Capt. Phillip had to put 'A Bounty' on his friend's head--

Later- after Capt. Phillip had left to sail home to England-- The new governor P.G. King- would not accept the damage or- The Killing of settlers caused by **Pemulwuy and** in 1801 gov. King *Actioned* the bounty-- and had **Pemulwuy** killed- journals said-a ships attendant known drinker- was attracted to-- The great Reward offered, which included 'Rum'--

So- he then shot-- **Pemulwuy**- who had become "a legend"- his gang was then led by His Son--called 'Tedbury'.
Pemulwuy was so well respected- that due to difficulty to stop him- he had been captured and escaped several times — when he had finally been killed — His head was then severed and Sent to England for autopsy- to help scientists- try to understand- why this <u>Superior</u> aboriginal was so hard to kill. His head has not been found since.!?
Capt. Phillip was recalled to England in 1792-- his friend Bennelong and His friend Yemmerrawanne went with him-- The Two lived with Capt. Phillip for many years- They were treated like Celebrities- they Toured England--met King George 111. Which hardly concurs with 'Activists Claim' that *"<u>We Fought them from Day One etc</u>'* – when these Men went to England to Live with "Their Friend" Capt. Phillip.? Colby had stayed with his wife. Later then Yemmerrawanne-- died in England — I have seen the photo of "an obelisk" as sits on his grave. But "The Elders" took advantage-- Telling all that wife and child- were **"killed"** by Capt. Phillip (died in hospital)-- <u>From my research</u>- I suspect: --It was that line of *Fight- drive the British 'killers' <u>from our land</u>*--as came from those

"Elders"- Who refused to meet and talk to Capt. Phillip-- That line as is likely behind most-- if not all- of the "porkies"--*as eventually led **to** 'the elders' **un-expected**- 2021 "Confession"* that "*we are NOT the Original owners*"--Albeit "the activists"-- Still claim to be "**First Nations** people"- here for 55,000 years- Others- including Our PM--in The NO Vote Campaign--were saying 65,000- or some did say 70,000 Years—It doesn't matter I SAY-- Pick A Number--any Number—Pick any Number-- To suit 'The Cause'.!

The irony is that—In all my research to study each slaughter or massacre claim including the 7 bodies as reported to have been Shot/Killed at "Waterloo creek"—The 28 be-headed at "Myall creek"- and 14 at Appen--**All on record**.

I Found--most other "Claims" were not supported by reports of bodies being found-- like when The Writer said *20,000 were slaughtered*—yet None of The bodies were ever found. It could also be seen—that it was in these writers books--where we did first learn of the most Dramatic and sensational **Frontier wars** and **the Genocide**—All of which have motivated Young aboriginals to seek their 'Revenge' Today--because they read *and see*--*Believe* all that *sensationalist* **Rubbish** writing- as The video and Movies **Crap--ALL Presented with NO Preface**.!

Oh yes--writers sold thousands of books- videos- movies etc. And they were also responsible for the Direction and severity- Of the aboriginal thinking and belief that all of this **Crap** as they read in those books/saw on Screens-- was True and it all was presented- Just **185 years after** it was Supposed to have happened.? So- we could be sure that those writers knew everything as they wrote about-- *was true*-- Huh.?

My research found that—all of such *'Genocide'* and all of the *'Frontier wars'*- as they wrote about-- likely *Never happened*— Anywhere- **EXCEPT- in their Books.!**

But this is what Aboriginals know--IS part of-- **OUR History**--

Yet still--in all the wars and genocide--they wrote about--
Surprisingly They did Not tell--where the Bodies were to be
Found.? **NO-- Bodies** of the slaughtered Ancestors--were Not
found--Nor were body- bones ever found — **I wonder why**.?
Then--I found it is ironic —
That the same writers did not write many books, if any with
their type of *made-up* stories --**About-** 'the Darwin war'--
Simply because writers couldn't '*sensationalise*' because all the
names of those who Fought and those killed- as with Their
Bodies--**are all--On Record**-- So there of course-- the scope to
write such '*made-up*' stories with the outlandish claims of like
20,000 were slaughtered (but No bodies found) IS not there-
which *should really*--Tell Readers-things about those writers.?
But as with the **"massacre map"** we are led to believe it is
ALL Totally *true and ALL correct*-- yet here--the reality is--
AS I Found:--
That IF just 20% of all of the massacre and slaughter claim
stories- **were true**- There would have Not only been 'bodies'
being 'Found' everywhere- also- They would know where
their Ancestors were Buried--But the most amazing things to
myself are that none of those writers- "activist" or "elder"
aboriginals--DID EVER seem to Do their own count —
None ever Tallied Up--their ancestor Numbers claimed to be
slaughtered--Never Compared Their Totals--against Numbers
known/assumed to have been Here Originally-- in 1788--
Where if they did Tally these Numbers UP — Then **Logic** Says-
There would be--NO aboriginals left-- after 75--100 years.!
But **None** seem to ever realise when to **Swear** that Thousands
of Their Ancestors were Slaughtered (as So many Do) **First**--
that they likely **would not have EVER had** *Thousands* —
In Their Line of Ancestry.? BUT-- **NONE** ever seem to Logic-
anything- like that.?
Then-- **None** talk about **"the Darwin war"** —

The Real War as turned out to be ***the most significant* event —** for all of The Aboriginals- where- when the Japanese army did attack us-- *in 1942--*
IF- *the British had not been here-* The Japanese army would surely have:--

massacred--The whole aboriginal race.!

But I am sure--the "*truth telling* elders" would NOT have told their young aboriginals- Their Stories- **about That War —** Because they could Only relay **"Facts"** or- '*the Truth*' — which- appears was never "their go".!
So- I say to Aboriginal people — now **HEREIN-- I write--**
To tell you about the Darwin war.! Yes- when you Open both eyes-- you will see clearly- that-- whatever you "**thought you knew**" of your aboriginal History- IS- just what *'the truth telling elders'* have Told you — in their many "*made-up*" stories as are made-up-- from a series of Other-- **made-up stories —**

   Same as- *"the Truth telling elders"- who:--*
      swore they were **Original** Owners —
      swore 1,000's- were *massacred"* at waterloo creek —
      swore there were **hundreds** run off cliffs by Soldiers -
      swore there was no in-breeding- no sexual abuse of
          their young girls--
      swore that whatever they told you was "the truth"--
      swore there was no need *'to take children'* from parents

When it was mostly **all false**- just their own *made-up* stories.!
Confirmed when they confessed of *"the mungo's"* in 2021 — But then "the elders"-still said- *we are owed* –as Thousands of our Ancestors were slaughtered by the British- but they just didn't tell--where all- The Bodies were buried- or what did happen to all the bodies of the Thousands killed/slaughtered- No — they just didn't tell them what happened to the bodies.?

Well—now that you all have your eyes Open—I will herein--
demonstrate why **aboriginals are:--**
  Not owed anything—and--
  Why--we--should be Equal--
Because--we all have been incredibly- Conned.!

As **FACT IS**—The British did Not "Steal" the Land—at First-
they came to Occupy a small area- to House their Convicts- to
teach them How to Live\Survive in This Small Settlement—
which took up just as much of this Land—
much as about A Part of what would be Our smallest Suburb
today--
But when Capt. Phillip saw the Primitive Lifestyle of The
Natives and How they lived- **He decided To Help them**-and
He Developed things for All to Share—
Which has been Helping Aboriginals ever since-Building for
ALL To Share—
Planning to be Equal—planning for those who worked to then
have Land to Build their Home upon—but as time went by—
we came to understand that whilst A Small % were able to
Study hard to gain their Education and some learnt to hold
White- and Blue-Collar worker jobs—some of the others could
'Find and Hold A Job'—
But a large % of those in the bottom part of The Numbers—
would be unlikely to want to Work and so would dwell on
Payments from The Government—to Live on Welfare.!

Here now I show you what I am talking about—because when
we **"compare losses"**- deaths activists _claim_ in Colonisation
and those later-- Killed as fighting to **SAVE** this country—
Fighting to **SAVE The Aboriginal Race--**

Here to demonstrate Loss <u>comparisons</u>

<u>The Tallies look much as below</u>:--
Fact- here <u>recorded</u>.   **Maybe-** <u>No records.</u>

<u>The "invaders"</u>-- and--   <u>the "aboriginals"</u>

loss boar war	**800**	**loss claimed in settlement**
loss ww1	**60,000**	**8,000**
loss ww2	**34,000**	At end colonisation-
loss pacific	**40,000**	20,000.?
Loss Darwin--1500		<u>No bodies but--</u>
and – growing--		<u>est. Loss 190,000</u> .
est. + **98,000** wounded		
large % died later.		**Say:--235,000** <u>Total.</u>
Est.= 235,000 <u>plus</u> wounded.		

The Tallies Show-- we-- <u>Should be Equal</u>.!

Australa fought in all those wars- to help Allies who would help us – IF we ever had a problem –

THEN--**we did have a BIG problem in the 1942--**
So – Here I say-- **we- should be Equal.!**
Because- it was NO *"invasion"* **of Australia in 1788.**
But **it was--**A Real *"Invasion"* **of** Darwin in 1942--
Yet The "elders" don't-talk about that-- I ask **Why.?**

Why – Do our Governments--Not talk about it.?

Yes-the 1942- *'Invasion'*- of Darwin- was **Real**.
we should be — Equal.!
Here- many aboriginals- joined "the British" and 'Allies'- to fight to **SAVE** Australia and--
> To-- **SAVE** the aboriginal Race--

So-- I say-- we should be — Equal.!

Those alive — wounded — killed — all On Record.

I say--We should have a Darwin War day.!

Because it is <u>incredible</u>- that-- as they sort out who was here First — and how many were slaughtered — in an Invasion-- that--**never happened.**! Here "the elders" and "activists"-- **Do not talk** of — or- acknowledge THE IMPORTANCE of-- the Darwin war — where in 1942--British descendants-- With aboriginals--and Allies--fought Together-- to repel the heavy Japanese army invasion--**of Australia**.
They **fought** — many died-- to SAVE Australia —
      They fought-- to SAVE the aboriginals-
Yet the aboriginals-- and governments- **don't acknowledge** their efforts in this war--as they waste so much time- effort- and money arguing about **the 1788- "Invasion" —**

That never happened-- I ask-- Why.?

Why-- do we **not Honour-- those brave people** who fought to **save us** from *the Japanese*--in Darwin in 1942.? Why have the aboriginals kept 'fighting' against the British regardless.? Against--all other Australians as they are being Paid by and using Benefits From--All supplied to them by-- The Government-- when at same time saying —

we want our land back-we want to have our culture when this Ideal is Not feasible- why do they not see that.?
Then — Why are the details of the Darwin war-- **All facts**--now Not being taught TO Our Children-- in our Classrooms — **Why.?**

Because- IT IS-- A BIG Part-- of OUR HISTORY.!

"Sorry"

I need to address Why-- I am "Sorry" also.!

Yes--to write a book as this about 'the aboriginals' — one-- could not think of doing this — and not include a part to confirm my personal feelings and to also say — 'Sorry'.!

But — my sorrow--

Is not as everyone else has been considering- no- my sorrow- is that my research has found--it is just so incredible that-- "the whole aboriginal race" — and the people led by our current PM — continue to "foster this growing division" of our population--why together — they will not make "A Stand' — Why they will Not **"draw a line" in the sand** (as 'they' say):--

To make a decision- stand up- demand stop- **define "Equal"** **S**tart with facts — as:--

> First — there was NO invasion in 1788 at botany bay — Where Capt. Phillip vowed to help the natives — and-- <u>he created</u>- housing- food supply- hospital- schools- education- defence- clothing etc.
>
> <u>Yes there were</u> un-necessary deaths- black & white — truth is-no one really knows what happened- or why. <u>But--IF</u> — as claimed- by aboriginals-- that so many thousands of <u>their ancestors</u> were massacred etc- Surely-logic says -They then- could not be here today- If thousands of their 'ancestors' had been killed-- way back then <u>Logically</u>--How could they be here- today.?

Then — I am so sorry — that literally all of the super-well-- educated aboriginals- the professors- titled and others-**do not- appreciate-** how they were able to be well educated- to have what they have--Yet "they" will not stand up and say:-- Hey — lookie here--**we could not Have Been so educated** IF-- The British were not here--as then — IF The British were not here — we would have been "Invaded"- earlier-- by likes of Japan- or China--where- without any doubt at all —

Our whole aboriginal race--
would have been wiped out.!

So its time we started to change:--
To appreciate Our Friends--and start to **"work together"** —
To find ways to help the vunerable aboriginal people —
realising The Govt- do now spend aver **$2.35** on the 3.3% of-
aboriginals--per **$1**- they spend on other 96.7% of our Total
Population. To appreciate all that- Capt. Phillip's promise to
All of Your ancestors — has been carried out — and so now we
should be looking Forward- to "working together"--
Our multi-cultural population moving forward — as One.!
To stop protests — realise that right from early days — you
have been mis-treated/mis-led and *'brainwashed'* by Your
Elders — as they were 'brainwashed'-- by <u>Their</u> "Elders"since
"forever"-- this being done ever so sneakily- most
importantly <u>**without their — OR your consent**</u>.! Ok Now: —
Once we have the 'super educated' elders admit these
things- Then educate the rest of their people to understand
it- this Country will-- suddenly become "a better place" for
all- and all will begin to understand that-- **we ARE Equal.!**
Now--**Yes it is true--**
<u>I am a long time expert</u> in the use of *"brainwashing"*-- have
used it for many years-- but my sorrow here is that the
Young Aboriginals have been blatently- badly misled- also —
misinformed- Totally disrespected and *'brainwashed'* — By--
their 'Trusted Elders' — <u>*the worst part being*</u> — they were Not
Told- by 'Elders' that they were being *"brainwashed"*.?
Yes — *'brainwashed'* by their so trusted "Elders" of whom they
have been led to believe- they are always <u>*"truth telling elders"*</u>
who would not tell them lies- fibs or 'porkies'-- huh.?
<u>Trusted elders</u> — who- have continually "used them" and
even though leading some to 'take advantage of British--
Schooling and learning classes- where many now--

Have become highly-- Respected Professors and have been Advisors to The Govts-- During the last 100+ years etc- as each had progressed in their chosen fields and grew their education — Yet each has still Remained- an "Activist"- still continued to help create the angst-- vitriol and agro — as "the earlier elders" had created--Here <u>as I see it</u>--many with their higher education levels and- earned positions of 'trust' — are all so Smart-- yet--None had ever said to their elders: *eg:-- I don't believe that was possible.?* None- have ever said:-- *"Hey- isnt it time--we all did decide to work together — Time to forget the 200+ years of agro" — Isnt it time that we stopped <u>'making up'</u> Stories.?* Isnt it time we admitted:--
That although we all say- we want to *"return to our culture"* that we really are now Educated enough to know that-- <u>we could not survive</u>- *could not live* as *our ancestors did- to "live off the land"*-- we now are Smart enough to know--to even try to do that- too many would die- <u>they just could not survive</u>-- and — although some of 'the elders' wanted us to continue their 'Fight' — to drive the invaders from our land — we are now Smart enough to see that *'this'* has brought nothing but un-necessary pain and frustrations. **AND Now- We ARE committed to Honor the Brave Australians Who Fought in Darwin — and** did SAVE Our Lives- from The Japanese.!
We are — 'the Super educated ones' — we do know that most of those 'Old Ideals'-- lost their probability and practability-- a long time ago-- where the reality is that- as <u>Capt. Phillip</u>- did say- at the start:--That he wanted to help us *improve food supply — improve housing and living standards*--include *a medicinal service/and hospitals* — teach us to become *better educated* — help us to *develop better defence* — to understand and believe that we could continue to grow and survive — that with our elders- ancient weapons of spears- nullas etc-- we now know this was <u>Idealogy</u>-- <u>completely gone wrong</u> —

So--we can now see—when we look past all "the smoke and mirrors" and the "activists" hoohaa-- as they continue to put out there—That we can see those wiser "elders'- likely from 'the gulf of- Carpentaria' Should have gone to meet with Capt. Phillip-- Should have said ok—we see what you are doing—planting crops- building etc—and although you work on just a small area--of this land—we can see and understand how you- The British can help us—we can see potential for what you have done here- to grow and expand that it is going to be real and will benefit our people--
We know your people will make profits—so we will agree to work with you/The British—IF you show us how we too will share the profits as you will make by using this land.!
We realise that 'you/The British' have come in peace, and— you will help us—whereas other countries may come and not want to help us—but instead will intend to wipe out our whole aboriginal race—and still be doing what you are doing here—and we will not benefit from that approach.!
In hindsight—As *the author here*--**I say-** if that had been done by the original 'elders' then not only would there be 'a large percentage' of those super educated aboriginals as we have now—but there would also likely- not be any living in the humpies and there would be 'no problems'. To learn trades would be the norm with younger aboriginals and most would then be "working" rather than "living off the dole"- or as it is called today- living on "welfare" payments- and of course there is very much more--so yes:-
I am very sorry--For the way younger generations have been led to believe that what *"their truth telling" elders* do tell them is always 'the truth' —when as I demonstrate herein-- they have proven to be more like- on-going 'porkie' tellers-- and herein I will also solve-*"the waterloo creek massacre"*-- Which is No mystery at all — *and* maybe I can also *help* —

The most outspoken voice of Ms Professor Lyndall Ryan- as well-- She boldly introduced her ingenious "massacres map" where she has "found" est.**174 massacre sites**--*that no one else knew about.*? Sadly too—she also 'found' NO bodies—Nor-- body bones.? Not at any of those 174 sites—**I wonder why.**? And as I read even on the 13/7/23—she too is still very— **Confused-** as reportedly- *using her own words-* I first read she believed Reports as said *was like 40-50 massacred at Waterloo Creek- to be right* —but-- as I was reading reports of-- "australian academy of the humanities"-- Here—it quoted ms Ryan saying- *"there were 200 to 300 aboriginals massacred at waterloo creek* (in 1838.) *Not a guess- but-"***a stated fact***". ?* Which is incredible-- this just confirms as my research shows not- only **uncertainty**-- but that even Ms Ryan has admitted that she can just "*make-up*" any numbers to suit the occasion and I say--if-- the esteemed Professor Ryan can be that vague when she is said to be "the expert" on this subject- it really proves--My Report was more likely to be "Spot On"- as I say the worst massacre in aboriginal history with all those many hundreds massacred-at "waterloo creek"- **IS—**

a great-- BIG "Furphy".!

Where as such--I can help here also by declaring that reports I found- Confirm 10-12 natives were shot- and **7** others were Killed by major Nunns group- and the 7 bodies were taken back to the colony- to prove Retribution had been completed for the natives who had--earlier killed 5 unarmed settlers.!

So—that's the simple/real answer—which then just says:- **There was NO massacre at waterloo creek**- on 26th Jan 1838 or any other date.!

Of course everyone is sorry for atrocities if and where they happened and that should be for Blacks and Whites- as were killed during Colonisation of Australia—

I say likely were-- killed 'unnecessarially'- as those 5 settlers and many others- also needlessly killed by the natives.

No Doubt some were needlesly killed also--by Whites too—

However- reading reports from way back—trying to understand more of "aboriginal deaths—

The word used most was *"retribution".!*

BUT NO:--

There was NO massacre at waterloo creek- on 26th Jan 1838 or any other date.!
The massacre-at *"waterloo creek"*- IS —

An "Elders"-- Great—BIG-- "Furphy".!

Return to-- "Our Culture"-

Looking from 2021-- when the devastating news of -- "the mungo's" being proven to have died here some **62,000 years ago-** when aboriginals always claimed to be **"original owners"** having been here **55,000 years**-- then- the Mungo DNA did not match with aboriginal DNA- Meaning the experts say the Last of **'the mungo's'**- had been here <u>at least</u> 7,000 years- before the aboriginals--which to me — now creates a constant nagging worry that--I cant get away from--being as how all the highly honoured--so well decorated historical writers and reporters each who have claimed to have known so much about their subject- yet their- in depth- 'research' which has provided them with the know how- to be able to write such long and detailed stories about *"the aboriginal history"- Some wrote 20- 30 Books-* and to have advised Our Governments on-going Incredibly has now turned out to be-- that **IT** was all really just- <u>***their own made-up stories***</u> written from messages of some earlier "elder" aboriginals — we now see were great tellers of own "<u>made-up</u>" stories- albeit I found many were great 'porkie' tellers also--

Yet — none of these- nor the writers mentioned that they also had known of **"the mungo's"** which I say-- means they too seem to have been <u>**conned**</u>- and or <u>**misled**</u>- by their "elders" even-- before any of them ever put pen to paper.?
Now:--

Capt. Phillip said--the landing in 1788 was peaceful- they had- exchanged trinkets -lay down their arms--sang and danced with the natives- then- some had dinner with Capt. Phillip and crew on his ship--

"activists" <u>of course</u> — say:- the natives were agreived-and fought from day one.?
Just-so many "<u>made up</u> versions."...
when the real truth- In 'Capt. Phillip Journals' was that:--

42

The British- on landing in Botony Bay in 1788- Could not understand how the aboriginals lived – we here in Australia today- **still can't believe-** how they lived--having been told how the aboriginals were "Original" inhabitants of this land- yet in all of 55,000 years occupation--this was what Capt. Phillip found – these were "the type of Houses or called just Humpies" as they built – for up to 10- to live in--

Yes--occupants for 55,000 years--and yet:-- they had not built anything permanent - so- yes this was-- "the housing" that --the aboriginal people lived in-- which was very different to what- the people from England lived in –
So in 1788 Capt. Phillip learnt they live in small communities they lived by hunting and gathering-- the men would hunt large animals for food- women and the children would collect fruit- plants-berries.
The aboriginal and Torres strait island communities say:-- *they only used the land for things as they needed-- for shelter, water, food, weapons. They never overused it- never damaged it. (source: skwirk.com.au). These details surely written by an aboriginal est. likely in 2010 on arrival of internet.*

When--the people in the First Fleet came here to Australia-- they came from a developed country-where these were the type of houses- British people had been living in- to rent or many would have owned —

The "activists" claim 'the First Fleet'--**invaded**-their land- stole their land--took **their culture — so they still** try to drive "the british" off their land — to re-gain **our culture**.!

This- is Sydney harbour today- 230+ years later.

samples of Melbourne--Sydney domestic units- 2000-

But "aboriginals" want to return to "our culture"

55,000 years-of aboriginal "culture"--

Spears--boomerangs--nulla-nullas--bow and arrows as throwing tools- <u>Hit range</u>- effective- to 35 metres-

This is "our culture".?
We want to return to:--

"our culture".?

I say:--it's really time to:--

"wake up"-

These are some of today's weapons...

Effective <u>Kill</u> range--to 500-- 1,500+ metres-

Return to--"our culture"--

I say that would be A Disaster--your family--could not survive if you were to "go back to-'our culture'- as most of your race would die if not being able to receive "the products" or health additives now accustomed to using in civilisation- as they have now grown used to consuming — go back to "live off the land" — yes — for a holiday either to live in the bush- or live in some motel with meals supplied — heating and/or cooling--then 'Go out' to experience the Old 'elders' ways-- then come back to the motel for tea and sleep — Be realistic — few of the over 40's could survive if they were forced to go back to-- *'live off the land'*.

Many would die also by choosing the wrong 'berries' to eat — as also the life expectancy would grow smaller — then without doctors, hospitals and other medical experts — all those over 50 could not handle this change — then when referring to the younger generation — those who have joined the workforce — have children at school and are buying a house- car or just any other normal things for How they are Living Now — of which They have included within the life they are now Part Of — They would not be able to make such dramatic change — Psychologically- No.!

However — as most would know — this statement about *"return to our culture"* — is just a misnomer-- because they know it is just all 'Smoke and Mirrors' — and nothing more than putting pressure upon Government trying to convince them to instigate some "land grants or titles or awards' or even to promote some form of "payments" for loss of land or loss of Ancestor lives etc.   Moving on--**First**- NO--there was **No 'Invasion'- at botany bay**--as there was **No "Massacre"-- at waterloo creek** — and now the aboriginals say they are not Original owners.!?

And- at the massacre sites there were No bodies-- found.!
But I say <u>the consolation</u> with this *massacre story* is that:--
IF--"waterloo creek--was the worst "massacre"-- it means *All other claims of* "massacres" are *just totally false*.?
Because the massacre at waterloo creek — **is** <u>"a Furphy"</u>.!
Which makes--all others--just '*<u>made-up</u>*' **'false' claims.!**
<u>The truth is that</u> —
No one knows what happened or why- back in the 1800's because none of them/others/us- were actually there.!
The aboriginals claim of a **massacre** of up to 1,000 at **<u>waterloo creek</u>** — yet in major Nunn's- report — he wrote a max 10-12 were shot- 7 others were Killed- and they took the bodies back to the Colony as proof — they had captured the natives- who had earlier killed the 5 settlers.
This 7 as Nunn's group Killed-- is what "the elders" then claimed as-- *the worst massacre* in aboriginal history-- **NO-they** didn't mention they *had- first- killed 5 settlers"* — *so* next generations only know of "**<u>A Massacre</u>**- Because that is only what they were *told*- By the "<u>*truth telling*</u> elders"--
Yes- those "*truth teller*" elders--who also <u>swore they were</u> the "**Original owners**" — who also "told the truth about the-- **<u>waterloo creek</u>** massacre.! Yes--their most trusted "elders".?
But in fairness:- I say at least '<u>Professor McGrath</u>'- She did preface Her stories to warn Hers were "*made-up*" stories and **<u>Not facts</u>** as she wrote with *historical imagination* and *narration* to create "a good story"-"a good read"-**<u>Not facts</u>**.!
The question is always — to know- when the writer begins to write their story- where their *point of view* aligns — where it… then comes from — because-- in every story-- The Author-- Must choose <u>*the point of view*</u>--from which their story is told- Which is an important decision because **the point of view--**

CAN-- *Vastly alter the story.!* So- on this subject--the type of their reporting - combined with—lecturing—writing books—projecting images-- and in fact-- all things done by the aboriginal history writers--have had the same *points of view*- and- always done without any type of-"a preface" as Ms. McGrath did put on her writing. Many others were motivating "the activists" trying to boost the numbers of their ancestors Recorded as were killed or-- they say slaughtered and/or 'massacred' -by the British—yet always with **No bodies being found**.? But yet- all are- so intent to gain empathy as recognition where I believe they wrongly — Are Following much of- "the stories"- as they viewed- read or heard- believing that to be written by such profound Titled "Expert writers" then they **must be true-**
Like when they were:--
    'Told'- about *"the invasion"* of the first fleet in 1788.
    When--there was no invasion.!
    'Told' of *the armed conflict* in Sydney-from day one
    when-- *there was no armed conflict-*
    'Told' of *the many* **slaughters** *of their ancestors-*
    when- *no bodies were found--to confirm that-*
    'Told' of- *the "massacre"* at **waterloo creek in 1838-**
    when *there was* ***no massacre--7 bodies found.***
    'Told' of the massacre of 60 by soldiers at Coniston
    when **there were no soldiers—no bodies found.**
But--NOT 'told' of the Darwin invasion when there **was one** and--I say--it is sad:—

That the elders have treated them like this--
Having myself just recently said goodbye to my dear 100+ yr. Old Mum — and later then- to her Two siblings- who both passed at 104 years of age. Each ever so proud to receive *'their letter'* of Congratulations - from "the Queen"--
before her own demise- later- RIP.
They marked the end of their era- in my family--all-- now resting with their parents--in the same cemetery with their families around them — where I can go say Hi to them at any time--put flowers on their graves--it's an empathy thing —
Is why — to me--it is just so sad"--
The elders" have created this **"Furphy"** --which I see is--
Keystone to the aboriginal life and their "dreaming" —
with their younger generations--always sadly--being totally *"brainwashed"—*
Here I should clarify my concern for these people is much deeper than can be conveyed within any book —
Because- I know them-- and I know how **the *"brainwashing techniques"*** work-- because--I have been trained with the use of ***"brainwashing"*--** and — still do use its techniques- for myself-- and to help others--So herein:--
I want to demonstrate some of the ways activists continue to grow 'the presence' of serious **"brainwashing"**--
to maintain pressure on "words as were spoken"--
but first: —

I stop for a moment — because:--

I want to talk to all of--

"the aboriginals" --

to You — One and all —

as I do ask--

"Hypothetically"-

What IF--

What--IF--<u>you could</u> --get rid of "the British"--
As you all wish to do — just like that.?

What IF- say- they/we- all packed up--ship off to England-- They- could take time to destroy everything that they have built--or — more likely--
To first- just transfer all Money and IT systems to England then sell off all the livestock to ship overseas- and–to use all the cruise ships and planes as are still idle — to-then literally - within a few months:--

To be able to — just — Get up — and Go.!

Yes- to be able *to Go – to just- "walk out".!*
So —
you "elders" and all-- your aboriginal race--

Will-- <u>***finally have your revenge***</u>-

You--would finally **have** "your" **Land--** back again--

Your **aboriginal race** would be the Only ones here--
<u>*on your Land*</u> –

you finally--have got your vengeance —

Forget about-- "the mungo's"--

you finally-- win.!

Now--your multi thousands of aboriginals--

Can-- do-- as you or/ they-- want to do.!

SO then-- what happens next.?

Yes--IF—we other Aussies--Did--just up and leave-
we left--the water supply—all vehicles—although petrol
will soon run out—
We left all weather protected buildings—left the banks—
who won't have money--as the ports who won't have ships--
but you won't want any of those-- anyhow--
We will have left all the food stores for you—stock will last a
few weeks-- although will soon run out—but--

You won't want them- anyhow--will you—

Because you will all now--"live off the land.?.!
Even all the Uni-Professors and their families--
The transport and education systems will be there—
but you can't use them-- without power-- or fuel--
But--*you don't want them either*--
You are going back to—"Our culture"--
You have all said that:--

So then--
what happens next.?
You have your land back—Call it as you will-

and-- come to think of it--

Now with "the British" Gone-- you "Elders"-

Have--no one to seek vengeance against--

So what will you "Elders" be doing from here.?

Well--we will have better building materials now
So – we can start to build better "humpies" –

From a barren area humpy to a tropical warm weather one--

We can hunt kangaroos—every day--

We can do Dances- do Rituals to honour the ancestors.

We can do our rock carving—leave messages

Australia art   aboriginal rock art Australia tell stories by drawings on rocks

We will be living from the land--

The 'Professors' will All be here — with us...
Prof. Ryan will Show us all 'The Massacre Sites'-

We will have our flag- Only-

the symbolic meaning of the flag colours--
(as stated by Harold Thomas) is:- **black – represents the**
Aboriginal people of Australia. <u>Yellow circle</u> – represents the
sun, the giver of life and protector. <u>Red</u> – represents the red
earth, the red ochre used in ceremonies and aboriginal
peoples' spiritual relation to the land.

Some will still want to stay in the houses--as we

have left--

"the Elders" will eventually agree--maybe.?

So now – after- Months of sheer bliss-

All living "the dream"--

All enjoying-- Our Culture--

We don't need to protest anymore

we can go back to living with our culture

WE DON'T HAVE TO WORRY ANYMORE.!

I say--what a pity — **Not One-** of those people —

Except The 'Elders' Can recall <u>the Darwin war</u> — Not one.?

Why should they.?
Because **now--**
 they don't need to protest anymore--

So all will be busy--working out what their family will decide to do- for the future--
Where to wander- next- to Build their Humpies- what part of <u>Australia</u>- do they wish to see- Next.?
It will not matter —

Because--the fact that **"mungo man"** was found to have died here **62,000 years ago** — like 7,000 years before We aboriginals had claimed to have been here That to us — now-- **means 'Jacks shat'** —
it simply means that "The British" <u>*have gone*</u>-- and:-

WE Don't need to Protest anymore.!

But Wait— wait on--

What was that.?

Hold On A Minute--

There is A Noise--

60

What's That Noise.?

ARE They-- Plane Engines.?
and--

What are those Other Noises—

They *sound like*...
Like—
Oh- Shat--Like "Gunshots" –

What the hell could that be--

OH---HOLY HELL-- You Yell--
"Find some Cover"--

Because--IT IS Planes-- AND--

They have **BIG-** RED- Dots *on each one--*

<u>Holy Hell</u>*—* YES It IS*--Its-*<u>The Japanese</u>*--*

They are Straffing all the populated Areas--Dropping Bombs on The Buildings--automatic Gunfire IS Going Off everywhere--
 There IS NO Defence--

What CAN we Do.?

*And--*NOW*-- Their Army-- are Landing on all of-- The Vacant Airfields and The Empty Freeways--*
Our FAMILIES are being Shot Down <u>everywhere</u>*--*

WHAT A MESS *— Bombs Blowing Up Buildings — Gun Fire--Grenades are Exploding--*<u>everywhere</u>*--*

Our People are being Shot— being "Massacred"--
Our Women and Children are Yelling and Crying-

They ARE Screaming— ALL Over The Place —

 They are being Slaughtered <u>everywhere</u>--

WE Have NO GUNS--

What Can we DO-

OUR Aboriginal Race IS being wiped Out.?

Anyone got some WHITE Flags.?
Will that Stop Them.?

No – No-- It's All--TOO LATE-
TOO LATE   TOO LATE

Its ALL – TOO LATE--
WE ARE DOOMED-
The Japanese ARE Here--

*Seems--It's Just what happened to DARWIN.
WE Didn't want to know about That—*

"The Elders" — Didn't Believe Capt. Phillip-
When HE-Said:- *we were prone to an Attack.*
*How Can we Get **"The British"** Back.?*
How Can we--

Get "The British"-- <u>To Come Back</u>.?

WHO- Should We Call-?

OH Dear--
I Do Now <u>remember</u>--
I READ somewhere--That--<u>Sometimes</u>--

You Should be <u>VERY</u> Careful--
OF what You--

DO really--<u>WISH</u>--For--
And Now--
We SEE How It IS-- <u>SO Very TRUE</u>.!

Hey--
WE Don't want to Be A Part of
"Jap-stralia" —

That IS--<u>IF We Survive This attack</u>--

WE Don't want The Japanese to be--

The LAST Owners of this Land--

SO — What Can we Do--

How Can we —

Get "The British" to come Back —

NOW.?

WE — DO Really NEED Them--

To Come Back--

Right— NOW.!

<u>To Re-Iterate</u>-- Our "Allied armies"- Fighting as One--DID stop Japan from Invading Australia-- In- 1942.? The US naval victory at the battle of midway, in early June 1942, removed Japan's sure path in- to invade Australia by destroying its main aircraft carriers.

The Torres strait is the 150 km of crystalline water that separates the southern coast of new guinea from the tip of cape York in Queensland.

During the second world war this shallow area of water dotted by coral cays and islands, proved to be a vital strategic point for the American and Australian forces pushing northwards through New Guinea.

By the conclusion of the first 12 months of the Pacific war, 830 Torres strait island men, almost every man of eligible age in the area, **would volunteer to serve their country.** Thus-formed-- ***<u>the Torres strait light</u> <u>infantry battalion</u>***, the only indigenous battalion ever to be formed in our nation's military history.

By July 1942, the Torres Strait company was utilised in a counter -attack role, still defending the previous positions against--**the invasion of the Japanese army on Darwin-- But--**

IF "the British"--"*invaders*" **had not been here in 1942— where-- if we** had not built a government--built Allies-- Increased population--built weapons--built-a defence force— able to train the Torres strait fighters-who "Combined" with- **All our Allies and together-- then--**

        We defeated--**the Japanese army.!**

So- I say-- Wake up-- to <u>the aboriginals</u>--its time--
    It's time-- to **re-think your position--**
It's time to change your *"<u>dream-time stories</u>"*-

Darwin--was-- *"An Invasion"*-- ON our home soil.!

Planes with bombs-- destroyed Darwin harbour-- the Japanese bombed Darwin and set the harbour alight- sunk 11 ships + Then destroyed 30 aircraft and Our total infrastructure- **Our defences were very badly breached etc**-- No--I do not understand why--a **"one nation"** web site or any other aboriginal propagander **would not** include some of these facts-- within their claimed **"Australian history"**--

The British have lost 5,000 in colonisation--

Australia lost 60,000 + 156,000 wounded in- WW1-

Australia lost 34,000 + 31,000 captured in- WW2--

The Japanese won "the coral sea" battle-- Australia lost 40,000 in- The pacific war. **Japan tried to invade australia- where we** Lost the Darwin harbour--all bombed/and ablaze 11 ships sunk- All lost-- 30 aircraft destroyed-- infrastructure all lost--we had All defences breached-- many lives lost. Australia lost 3,000 + wounded in- Darwin war—

Yes--Darwin--was-- *"An Invasion"*--

A Tank from darwin war.

I say- wake up- to all Governments-

Darwin--was-- *"An Invasion"*--and I ask--
How could anyone in their right mind--**not imagine-**
what would have happened--to the aboriginals with spears &
nullas-- fighting the Japanese army.?
SO- I Say--**It's time:--**
To make "dreamtime" be **factual** and **grateful.**!
It's time to show some strength — show some "balls"-- show
some leadership and direction for-- **the indigenous people —**
it is time to train--meld them into society-- time to teach them
our **"Real Aussie story"** and way of life--of how true-blue
Australians- conduct themselves--
It's time to propose **"a history book plan"** for school children --
to include **both** aboriginal culture and Australian history--from
what has been built.! Not with "made-up" facts of massacres —
that most likely--may not have ever happened.!
It's time to have- guts- to insist on teaching **the real story** of
how everyone is Sorry — for the way it all began — **we DID all
make mistakes —** it's time to realize that the so-called writers
made up versions--of Our History- **are--** utter crap.!
They are "made-up-stories"- showing/sending all of the
wrong messages--
It's time to combine a small indigenous motif on our flag--
in one corner of our national Australian flag--

we are as "One Nation" — IT's called Australia.!
With the aboriginal flag separate--we are **a divided** nation.!
I say--like **now —** it is "the right time" **to wake up- the--**

Right time to change your *"dream-time stories"*.!

It's times like-in 1942--when the Japanese landed at Milne bay- that-'the whole indigenous people'-- **should ALL listen & understand**- **How in Feb.1942** the Japanese bombed Darwin and Broome- they "**massacred**"--160 'lark force' **aussie prisoners.!**
Our air force held them back- then they started another Invasion via the northern territory- to come overland via-- **the Kokoda trail--**a combined aussie milita- repelled the Japanese--**we Won--**but-we lost **72,814 killed + 31,000 were wounded** incl. Aboriginals but then on "the Kokoda trail"- our 39th battalion- Papua infantry "maroubra force"- **Helped by 'fuzzy wuzzy's'**- staged a huge battle-and together Repelled the Japanese.
Again- I ask "the indigenous" people--
did your *"elders dream-time stories"*- **tell about this.?**
Did they tell you how--to imagine/ **shock horror--**
What if-The British had not been here--What IF *'Japan had* **SUCCEEDED-** *What If They HAD Invaded"* taken your land.?
If you had no British/Aussie Army here to save all of your people- would **the aboriginal race** have made **"Friends"** with the Japanese--One of the cruellest army victors known.?

You should think about that.?

Yes-- **I Do** know the answer already.!
Here now--I have uncovered even more mysteries--with even more questions- more "wondering" with more of everything.! **Yes- my research** in this direction has resulted in another world of mystery and intrigue- beginning with wondering--**Why-the Hell--**wouldn't the Australian population be made aware of ALL of these details.?
The first item being--that I as many Australians would not have been aware of- That each time- we sent our armed forces into one war zone after another--I have now learnt—

That those armed forces--had included hundreds and even some Thousands of Aboriginals- who had volunteered and would-- have been fighting alongside our Aussie fighters-- Some- would not have gone overseas- and--would be restricted to help at home as well--and as their friends--in the wars- the aboriginal race did lose sons and daughters in their endeavour to help to defend our great nation.
So--**why don't the "activists" relate to these things.?**
Which in itself--poses a surprising revelation to prove that in-the main--most of these thousands of aboriginals had seen War--seen and been trained to handle Weapons--and from as far back as from World war 1 (ww1) would have learnt how to handle these weapons--how to use them to ward off an enemy--to have seen the destruction from those wars--
Yet "the elders/activists" did not learn from them.?
They have done this--right through to our latest and biggest saga in defence of Australia-- in **the Darwin war**—where--as **Captain Phillip had** *said* :--
the country was vulnerable to an attack. **AND** The Japanese army eventually did invade—Yes- they did Attack Did push into Australia at Darwin--and we fought them off- fighting with Allies to fend off the Japanese invasion as the combined Australians armed forces.!
***But- Question IS--**what if:--*
"the invaders of 1788"-- Families- **were not here.?**
The Japanese army **would surely have**--
 wiped out-- the entire aboriginal race.?
I ask- again--
Did the *"truth teller elders"* ever tell about that.?
My guess is--NO.!
So I say 'Elders' as Governments need to wake up.!

You Need to grow some "balls"-- You need to--join all of this History in together-- then-use it- to educate our children in their schools--
Not be feeding them totally bias aboriginal "made up" Crap-
Not Their 'rubbish' history — as written by some of those "pretend"or "made up" *would be*- aboriginal writers —
Yes we need to teach Our Children all of--**the Real Facts —**
Things we can Prove-- not made-up stories- NOT The Crap that Elders and The Writers have Featured- for 2 Centuries.!
Its ODD- that for all of these years "the activists" have been malaigning the British/Aussies--**the aussie armed forces —**
YET—

These are The People who Fought to SAVE Them.!
I First did not understand why "the Elders" did not mention anything about "the battle of Darwin" — **On our doorstep--** where Total casualties were- reported as 72,814. and 31,000 Aussies became prisoners-of-war--to die later.
Over 100,000 casualties--killed by the Japanese; and by end August 1945 over a third had died in prisoner-of-war camps.
BUT The Simple Logic is:--

Here- They could Not *Make-Up* their False Stories--
BUT Truth IS--
"The British" via Captain Phillip decided to Help The Natives AND have been protecting/ Saving the aboriginal Race- ever since-- as with some of the aboriginals who had fought and helped save us all--from the Japanese invasion-
Yet--this was not important enough to rate any mention--
by the then Prime Minister — when--
He decided to say His--Political **"Sorry".?**
Nor by any of the "Elders" — in their "dream time stories"--
 Nor by any of the "activist groups".!
 When **Yes--**

The Darwin war was *"A Real Invasion"*

I ask again:-- could anyone in their right mind —

Not imagine-

What would have happened —

To the Total Aboriginal Race-

IF —

the SO Called-- "Invaders" of 1788 --

Descendent **Families —**

Had NOT Been Here--

What IF — They-- were not here--

DID — You-- "Activists"--

Ever think — about That.?

THE Moral behind This Part — IS that:--

WE NEED each other

WE Should ALL be Acting as **ONE Country**--

ONE Multi-Race Australia

ALL Combined-

AND-

We Should **All Celebrate** Australia Day-

Just as-- We Should ALSO--

ALL — Celebrate —

A--DARWIN WAR Day.!

Celebrate Them--

"Together".!

Now-- as we take "A Breather"---

LET Us--Look at—

Some of 'Author Kev's'--

BACKGROUND--

And-

HISTORY--

My Background- **Briefly--Ok** — *Now at this point* — maybe my reader- will have decided to believe my writing — and-- My Thoughts of Logic — or-- maybe not.!
So- for me to start- to dispute any of the claims- as will be done herein — maybe they will label me- as 'Racist' also.?

So before I do that--I should tell my readers a bit of my background — so as- when I do make a statement — readers will know and understand- I am not just blowing off hot air- for example:--

big holes are needed to be dug- to bury bodies-- I have lots of experience digging holes. Being A Builder — back in the 50's- there were no power tools- no post hole diggers, and —
at age 15-to 19-- I built 9 country houses — mostly on my own — sometimes had help to lift walls — like when I built a new house for My parents, dad helped. (had electrician too.)

For each house--there was an average of 36-45 stump holes which I had to dig x min. 600mm deep- to stand stumps in- before could begin to build — my normal tool kit included- Crowbar to dig and Shovel to clear dirt from holes. If to do fences needed to dig post holes est. 3-4m apart on average 800mm deep.

Many years later — at our farm I had to dig a big hole to bury one of my horses — she fell and broke her hip - had to be euthasised — so even with a back hoe — to dig that hole then settle the body down--to back-fill- to cover the hole in- was a huge task. Then to be sure we had plenty of water for my then 36 horses — using my backhoe--I dug the existing dams deeper-- then dug 3 new dams — was a massive undertaking. Family pets as passed — I always would dig a hole with a shovel to bury them- to be close to us. **So-** when- I critise statements by writers as they **relate to Guns-** well —

I was a good shot with my .22 rifle — before I went to do National Army service training at puckapunyal vic.
Eg:- Building one house on a block at Marong- est. 20+ klm from home — as I sat to eat my lunch — I'd nail small drink bottle tops on fence posts- or big tree trunk — and during lunch — I practiced hitting these at 25-to 50 paces. To recall one day- there was a large Black Crow — high up in a tree-- way down at end of the paddock (*crows peck eyes out of ewe or lambs*) So I line this bird up- aim up high and fired-- <u>it was unreal</u> — *there was a pause* — then-- the crow just toppled over- -and fell to the ground — a great shot.!
We always hunted rabbits- before myxamatosis.
Then at Pucka we were taught to use many guns —
I was then a good shot with a .303 rifle. Did get a blast one day on the range as-- I was set to win *'the silver rifle'* contest — but my mate in next lane — he hadn't even hit his target with 10 shots — so in next round he found a bull and 2 inners on his target — he was rapt he had hit his target- the sarg didn't see the Matey side, as I didn't win the contest — later again--with friends- I flew up north-on a wild pig shoot pigs were destroying their family property landscape — my friends were keen shooters- had high powered rifles with telescopes fitted they had an old .303- and an old shotgun-- This day the pilot asked if he could have the .303- that left me with the shotgun- He was a great shot, with no scopes- then after they had shot a few pigs — we were walking along an old dry creek- my two mates with their big rifles are about 1.5 m apart and I was in the middle — walking half a pace behind them. <u>Suddenly</u> a big Black Boar- with big sharp tusks- burst out of rushes and is charging straight at us — the two riflemen had no hope of lining him up- so at about Two metres--I fired both Barrels- into his head- Stopped him dead--The Boar--fell at our feet —

Yes they sure blasted me-- for shooting when I was so close to them — but, we would have been gored--if I hadnt acted so quickly. So yeah — I do know a thing or two about guns and damage- they can do. In such a situation a skilled aboriginal warrior- <u>Could</u> have dropped on his knee--had the boar charge onto his spear- the momementum would have knocked him over- but he could have killed the boar — the un-trained marine with a 2 shot blunderbuss — most likely would have been gored- same as I and my mates would have been — <u>IF--I hadnt shot the boar</u>. But that didn't show up when they posed for a photo- with their foot on the dead **B**oar--to show--**Our** prized kill.?

At Our Farm- we had lots of vermin- 'they' said I could legally shoot them but--could not take them to "the knackery" I had to bury them.? Snakes- yes- but I just made a keen edge on my spade — one swipe- and off with heads — No snake problems.!   **Now my reader** has seen that- my writing — my thinking--my life--is not that of the Educated titled historian writers who have for decades been writing of this aboriginal subject-writing as I say-misleading-*"made-up"* Stories — **Not facts.!**

Myself — first born of Four- to lowly paid country couple- who dedicated their life to care for their 4 children to obtain the best Public school education possible. My schooling-- well — First State school- then Tech school--where The Educ. Dept. Stuffed up-as 'they' decided- all country tech schools should have Exams set in melbourne- no checks first-- to see where we country schools were at- Result being that my class had not seen material we were to provide answers on- so a whole class- is guessing answers to un-seen subjects- just the '3 brains' got 50%+ myself next at 48%-and later given "a pass" I was disgusted.? Sure it would be same at end of year-- So at age 14--I Left Tech school immediately--

Much to the chargin of my parents. But I had found a job — to learn To be a carpenter — Learn how to build houses.

Sadly just same 3-- Did pass end of year exams- A Disaster lost year for my whole class--but I had a job- and I learnt how to build houses I did build my first house at 15- to help a neighbor--later at 17- I was A Builder who rode a pushbike — towing a box of tools- on wheels- behind my bike- and there I built a total of 9 of those 'Country' houses- and lots of reno jobs. Till then being Conscripted to do Army Training at puckapunyal in victoria there to be appointed 'Builder' to update Army training circuit at Puckapyanyal. **The significance** of mentioning my building and the Army- was that way back there in 'the 50's' we had none of todays docking saws, nail guns or power drills — no augers on backs of tracters- till many years later- so to build a house-I first had to dig stump holes. I had a crowbar to dig and a shovel to clean holes out, for every house — then to use other end of bar to tamp the dirt in around stumps.! No- I only had hand saws, hammers hand drill, chisels and crowbar/shovel etc — Today--I watch in awe of builders- and how they use their nailguns- docking saws- portable power saws- drills etc — even had 8 ft pine studs as I had 9 ft heavy hardwood studs. **And also-- from my Army training--**I am very **suspicious** as to how- a marine/or Settler untrained in using the 2-shot load-tamp-long barrel- Bessie blunderbuss gun which reports said were just 50% accurate used by _Trained_ soldiers. But when writers said--_they just shot them dead — slaughtered them all--_ which means 300 to 1,000 shot in the head-or in the heart by un-trained 'shooters' where my view would be-- **that's like--**Total Rubbish.! But there-- the problem was — No One queried that Incorrect statement.?

The next thing IS- I do believe that I must write this book — **I Must write my story**-- because I see--it is important, and: —

Because--**Someone does <u>need</u>- to say something**
But--I likely will be called "Racist" — because — I don't like one sided un-challenged commentary--as we have here-and- I believe it is time that someone called these people to task — As I herein intend to do.! Writers who tell "<u>*made-up*</u>" stories or "untruths" without a qualm just annoy the hell out of me. Provided they sell many books and videos is all they care of — where- as I said-- I have found just one- <u>"*Professor McGuire*</u>"- who, as others--I will also be taking to task- but she at least did *<u>preface</u> her book/s* by saying--"*I write using my historical imagination--and narration — to create a good read*"- *to write a good story- not facts.* But **problem is —**
I found no other writers who did do that.! <u>Albeit</u> it's much like "the warnings on cigarette packs" — people still smoke — and still seem to die from effects of smoking.? *(I actually tried it- gave it up at 12- wasn't for me.)* <u>Same as here</u>- aboriginal readers- still believe her "stories" were true.? **No- I am not racist —** I say-we should be sharing--should forget about 'them & us' **racist rubbish** <u>Myself- No</u>-- **Not racist —** I-- had 'aboriginals' in my grade in State school--in Tech school my mate was a China man--had other nationalities also played in my sports teams--later had other China man- in my squash team. I was holder of most Pennants won as Captain and Coach at Doncaster vic.! But none were ever selected to be in my teams or — not--because of their- Nationality-- they were in my team because they wanted to play squash and-- did accept my coaching them to win- more often than be beaten.
<u>Our opponents</u> were Australians- Italians- Greeks- Germans- and other different races-- and there was always harmony-- and respect.! All did join for drink and eats- after each match win or lose.? Our neighbours were Italian and Greek - Many who became lifelong friends- some RIP.!

We still go put flowers on their graves. Their children have also-- Continued to Be Friends with our children/grands but- in all of the years — We presented our own versions of foods as our parents taught us to grow and cook to eat.
We also shared birthdays- weddings- funerals and meals- at each other's homes--**Yet at no time**- except to *rib one another* about habits, our expressions, footy teams etc. There was **never** any 'racism'- no-- none were ever seen to be "racist"- we really would not have known what it meant.! Every one of these people were just **"Australians"**--some were better players- some just became more wealthier than others- had more children than others and yet it never altered how we felt toward each other-- nor were there angry situations- as are so often seen today — often as result of "a racist comment".? No- "my people" were **just "Australians"** and happy to be such--happy to learn from each other.!
Then also--
I did spend 30+ years in "Specialty Sales"- after I first did **EB** (encyclopaedia Britannica) **Sales/motivational training** to learn how to sell encyclopaedias-- where I learnt all about *"brainwashing"* — learnt- the **"techniques"** which helped me sell EB-then S/Steel cookware- finance- cladding- used cars- home reno's- design/sell kitchens- heating--air-conditioning etc- to many Nationalities- City white/blue collar workers Country folk-- low-income people- farmers- some in Politics- Govt. workers- Doctor- Council engineer- Religious minister.
Then later--
we had 3 Retail shops — serving many races-yet No-not ever racist--I played football- bowls- cricket- squash with many nationalities and during all those times--would have heard none of the racist remarks Said to be made to 'aboriginals' today — which I feel are mostly imagined or- misinterpreted- or- over "exaggerated" by the way too Sensitive aboriginals--

82

Of today and <u>recently</u>--I did actually send a Text <u>to now</u> retired footballer--**Eddie Betts**- To say:-- *Eddie-loved to watch you play football mate- loved what you have done--now don't spoil your image and do or say things like your friend has done--I wish you well mate--* but- do say--*I agree with 'ole Sam' (Newman) as he said--the crowd didn't boo your friend because he was 'an aboriginal' or because they are 'racist'--No--they booed him because he acted like <u>a dick head</u>* -- I add- all admired him playing football- congratulated- applauded 'achievements'- but then he turned sport into "Racism" even made gestures as if he were an aboriginal <u>warrior</u> and wanted to attack a spectator-- a young girl as called him 'a name'- it seemed- at a football match - <u>for god sake</u>--**No it was not racism--** he used his position to 'make a statement' same as when he was presented with a very prestigious award — again — he decided to "push his-racism and politics"--**No- sorry- not on.!** No- in all my years playing sport- often called names — but- sports players do that-- to try to put an opponent off — but-- not as racist--that's just competitive sport.!

Then- <u>also those 30+years of sales experience</u>- took me inside Thousands of people's homes and offices- in cities- country- and in sport centres-- but wherever — No--"racist" was <u>not</u>-- ever used.! Yet--today so much is being said and presented in public and in particular on aboriginal websites —
by the people who all now seem to want to create and <u>foster</u> "Racism"--**to me- NO--sorry--not on.!**
Here it really **does not- nor--should not--exist.!**
<u>And- aboriginals</u> — well I have seen them from many angles--been where they live- played sport with them--have visited their homes in the city--been where they built their 'humpies' — watched as they collected their pension $$s —
Paid their debts etc- albeit--some areas didn't pay — sent my friend broke in His General store (rip RF.).!

And--I am likely one of the very few alive today—at least in Australia who has been trained and practiced and am fully--Experienced in- *the Power* of EB "**brainwashing**"- and— **The Techniques** within--so I am well versed to be able to explain how _Powerful_ this medium is-- and how Strong it can be--which is--what I have seen being used by these "_truth teller_ Elder" aboriginals-- to guide and control direction of younger generations- using the power of *"brainwashing".!*
So my story here then-
Has been partly taken from my long life-- from what I have read-- from 'the net' where I read what aboriginals genuinely seem to believe has happened to their people- which I say is sad- because today-young aboriginals don't _understand_ or _accept_--that most of their "angst and mental confusion" has been- and still is--being created by the "_truth telling_ elders" as they love and trust the most- coming to them in "*the _made-up_ stories*" as their trusted "elders" were "_making up_" to always be presented "**as Facts**" which sadly--young generations—Naturally-- all have believed.!
The early literature- the books/movies and videos-- all--were just--so well presented- yet all were *"_made up_ stories"* which they all have- sadly believed <u>were true.!</u> Because the "elders" told them so--presenting it in *"dream time stories"*.! All of which is why they do believe they are '**Owed'** because **their elders-** told them so.!
Yet--they also told them- we are "the _Original_" Owners of this land--we call Australia- and--sadly for most—they have "believed" _without question_ what they were told- because if it came to them- from their _trusted_ "elders" — then **it definitely was True** which is why- **the internet** has become a huge vehicle for-- *"the activists"* who still campaign to promote 'the truth"- that Thousands of their aboriginal ancestors were **massacred--** By Colonisation- <u>as example:--</u>

On the Internet Recently- I perused what became <u>Hundreds of "entries"</u>-- which also Included Professor *Lyndall Ryan's* book- along with other writers books—
Of which all were focused on proving **"Massacres"**--
All Sadly which many thousands of people- now around the world- are reading--yet no one stops to think-- no one asks or considers--that all these hundreds of **massacre site entries** would have Only been listed on The Internet-- <u>After</u> 2010— and entries describe what happened <u>at That site</u> **200+ years ago**—listing this as Clear and Concise- as if this was really 100% accurate and truthful—which could only have been listed by some aboriginal 'Activist'-- keen to promote their agenda's-- **None of course stop to consider that-- IF:**—

    Yes--**IF <u>even</u> 20%** of those entries <u>were</u> True then-- <u>Obviously</u> there would have been **No aboriginals left after the First 75 to 100 years.!**
Likewise--None could have been here today- to be able to write those Internet Entries in 2010—Because their quoted losses by far "Outnumber" <u>ANY total</u> of their aboriginals as claimed to have EVER been here on this land.?
Which prompts me to ask- again—IF then those 100's of "massacre" claims- were correct—ALL the 'Ancestors' Dead-
    <u>Who then wrote the entries in 2010</u>.?
    When all of their ancestors-- Had ALL been Killed--
    How did these people get to be Living here in 2023. ?
<u>Herein</u>—I explain how I do understand their direction—but to write and lodge such entries- claiming such losses--no matter how 'Illogical' it was- as I will show later- it makes **"A Farse"** of whatever they- <u>are trying</u> to prove.?
Yet--my story is not so much to be arguing about all of that-- <u>Rubbish</u>--but to tell my readers--being <u>a constant</u> user/and believer of **"Brainwashing"**- then I do understand—and have found that *"dream-time stories"* have always been the--

Most **Powerful influence**--upon aboriginals and their thinking-- Right to today- So I write to show my <u>unbiased</u> Research-- Has found enough to be able to confirm —
That I do believe:-- the aboriginals of last 200+ years--*have - been used*- and still- here today-- they are **being used** — By their most trusted "*truth telling* elders"--where often unwittingly' they are still being told "*made-up* **stories**" that are **Not true** — they are being Sold- a great BIG "on-going"- Furphy- By-and from--their **trusted** "elders"--which means unfortunately — then in turn--**that all of us Australians –** The 96.7% Other part of the Population are also being **Sold-- a great "BIG** Furphy".!
Because my 'research' found an almost *"underground like-- terrorist" type movement*--except not being built- *"underground"* it is happening *right before our eyes* — and IT — IS also being mostly paid for (shock-horror) by Subsidies or-- In Other words--By our **Australian Govt. funds.!**
And even worse- to me is--I did not read One--of the many aboriginal based-web sites--that had--even One complete paragraph--to say —
How their **brave aborigines** had *fought with* (not <u>against</u>)-- their **fellow Australians to win--**

the Darwin war.!

Yes- they fought <u>together</u>- to **SAVE Australians** --

They *fought* **together** to **SAVE** the Aboriginal race.?
Others did write books about it--but not--the "activists"-- Not one aboriginal "activist" reporter-- did--write much of-- the "Invasion of Darwin- in 1942."--
 The "Invasion"--*that did really happen*- and-- where here "aboriginals" did also fight-- some had also died--Yet none of the activist "Elders"--thought it was "a big deal"--Or thought IT worthy of even "A Mention" —

Not one of the "expert" aboriginal "activist" reporters -has--
Included this in-- as they wrote about aboriginals **lost** or —
being **killed by the British**--of "the first fleet".?

No--all of that they were writing- was solely to prove —
how many *Thousands* of aboriginals were *"massacred" by--*
'the First fleet'-"the invaders"-- 'the British'-
(now our government) —
So--
I have come to believe the problem with aboriginals —
IS Simply that:--
    They *don't want to understand* —

    They *don't want to believe* or ever accept- that —

    Their trusted *"truth telling elders"* –

    Have been *"brainwashing"* them —

    That Their- *"truth telling elders"* Have been –

Feeding them "Made-up Stories" –

Literally-- forever.!

My History-
The Author — cont.

"My History" —

MY Family--and myself--
Because WE-- DO Have "HISTORY"--
From way Back as:--
MY Ancestors First Landed IN Victoria--
They Ran A Coach Service--
In 1878--from Lorne — to The Geelong-Train-

LORNE Vic.

There was NO-- "Great Ocean Road" Yet--

So-- They Ran The Coach Service --
From Lorne to Meet The Geelong Train.

LORNE Victoria

ALSO—NEWS From --**WAY Back--In LORNE—** in 1984--

Says- The "Ladies" of MY FAMILY-

Were involved here: --In December 1894 the South Australian Parliament became the first in Australia, and only the second in the world, to extend the suffrage to women.

The 1894 Petition was presented to Parliament on 23 August 1894, just as the third reading of the Constitution Amendment Bill, proposing to extend the suffrage to women, was being debated. It contained 11,600 signatures, two-thirds of them from women, and was the largest of several petitions presented on this matter.

The Petition was the work of a group of women's organisations, the **Women's Suffrage League**, the **Woman's Christian Temperance Union-** and the **Working Women's Trades Union**, which gathered signatures from all over the colony, campaigning for the suffrage as they went.

The 1894 Petition was recognised at the time as a significant factor in securing the passage of the Constitution Amendment Act (1894/5) and can be regarded as an iconic document of the 'first wave' of **the Australian feminist movement.**

My Ancestors--
Helped Start-THE GREAT OCEAN ROAD-at Lorne.!

Picks and Shovels--No Dozer-- No Mechanical Help
Back then-- *Details:-- Otway-life magazine—*

Lorne

VIC 3232, Australia

IN Early Days 'The Mountjoys' (My Ancestors)
provided up to 40 Beds for Holidaymakers at Lorne

Before they Later **Built Erskine House — ABOVE --** which is now Owned and been Up-Dated to be-- **"The Mantra"** Holiday House.

LORNE.

The First Horse Drawn Passenger Coach in Victoria--
A Service from Lorne to link with the train--from Geelong--in 1878, with the ever- increasing rise in tourist numbers-- Caleb and Thomas Mountjoy-- established their coach service to bring the visitors from the Melbourne train- to Lorne.

After breakfast in Geelong and two more train changes at-- Birregurra & Deans marsh where lunch was enjoyed at Bell's Hotel-- passengers then undertook a two and a half hour- dusty and hot coach journey for the final twenty miles to Lorne.

In its heyday—
Ninety horses were used in the service and eight men were engaged in the blacksmith shop at Erskine House.

<u>Some of</u> "**my personal Background**"-which apart from my marriage and birth of our 3 children and sport in Bendigo. My life has been one of maturing--evolving--within an ever- changing world- taking opportunities as they appeared as eg:--First-- due to <u>a stuff up</u> by Education dept. as 'someone' had decided mid-year--country tech schools should have their exams set same as Melbourne senior schools — <u>Without first checking</u>-- where we- country schools- were all at--we had not seen the material used for the exam--I was given "a 48% pass"-so <u>disgusted</u>--till I saw just top 3 had got 50%+- we were all guessing at answers to un-known subjects- So--at 14--I left school immediately--I knew it wouldn't change quickly. Sadly- same result came for my grade of 30+ pupils at end of year- again top 3-- to be only ones to pass--I hated to think of "the future" for all of those kids.!?   <u>But I had a job</u>-- with A Builder to learn to build houses--   Then at 15- I built a house for a neighbour-- became A Builder at 17-- built 9 houses in the local area- incl- a new house for my low-income parents-- at 19 building my first brick-veneer home- when Conscripted to do 3 month- **Army-national service training-** in "assault pioneer corps"- there later- to be appointed as Builder to up-grade Army training course at Puckapunyal vic.

I mention my army training--with the 'other things' as I feel <u>are relevant</u> herein — **because-**doing national Army service- I fired hand-guns- 'repeater'-- auto gun- .303 Rifle on a range — and the Bren gun etc. **I was a good shot —**

Due to win *"the silver rifle"* on the range- but a mate wasn't much good with a gun- 10 shots and he hadn't even hit his target. So <u>suddenly</u> he had a bull and 2 inners with last 2 clips- *he was rapt*--well — I didn't need a *'Silver rifle'* anyhow- but I got a blast from 'the Sarg'-- but--<u>what are mates for</u>.? So yes- I know of guns and have used and thrown a bayonet- and grenades- killed a wild boar with a shotgun — and sure do — know what it takes to 'bury' bodies like to dig a hole to bury one of my horses- was a massive job- even with my "Backhoe"--still it was a hell of a job--then to build 3 dams with my Backhoe was a <u>massive task</u> even to dig holes deep enough to bury a pet cat or dog with a shovel--is hard- even when can choose where to dig.

Now--I clarify--before my reader gets the wrong idea--
<u>I tell you these things</u>--only so you know that when I write *my opinions* about such 'reports' or 'comments'-- that **they are real-** because I have found on this aboriginal subject which I am trying to write "my story" <u>around</u> — so often-the-- *"irresponsible comments"*-and *"impossible claims"* <u>abound</u>--like- *"they slaughtered hundreds — shot them all"* which when I then label that as *<u>"impossible"</u>*-- my reader does know--that I am not just--talking through *the back of my neck-* or--making wild statements--like as again I read- someone wrote recently-- <u>to re-iterate</u>--*"the mass grave of 300+ aboriginals just hasn't been found yet.?* Here--**in my opinion and experience – that is such--** *"a ridiculous statement"* — yes- I do relate to 'the grief' — but that person is talking **Crap** and-- has no idea of the-- **Mammoth task** it would have been--to dig such a hole-

With no shovels and no Backhoe- to bury 300 bodies--then cover them in—so that the bodies would not be un-covered by natural rains. Well to me--that person- has likely never even dug a hole to plant flowers in some soft soil--to know- just *how **impossible*-** that task would have been and as such how *ridiculous*--that statement is. Then-- how *naïve* it also is-- to expect people to believe it could possibly be "true" **Here- the mystery to me is** — that it is able to be "Printed in a daily newspaper".? Where- many thousands of people can read it. **And** of course-would know it is True when- it is printed— yet- **it likely came- in** *"dream time stories"*—came from our *"truth telling elders — and it gets printed in the Daily newspaper Hey — this must be true- Right.!?*

So--this is the type of 'reports'- 'statements'- 'comments' as I have frequently found relating to "the missing bodies" of the many *thousands* of aboriginals-- as are **said** to have been *slaughtered* and *massacred* --right from start of settlement of the colony--of which I am trying to address--herein.?

So--my story is directed to all readers-- but in particular-- *to all aboriginal / indigenous-* to say yes- I do relate to 'the grief'—and I personally have been forced to depths of utter despair *(harassed till set to head butt a train)-***luckily- somehow- I didn't.!** Then I had 6 family-and several of my friends pass-- in the early 'Covid' years. When sadly could only attend just- 2 of the funerals to send them off to their future resting place -

It was very sad--each time.

However- my story here is about- **"the aboriginals"** -- **It's their story"**--from start to end—but those are the type of "Factual" statements and the many "made-up" stories and comments--I have needed to try to-- "sort out"-- to browse through-- to first try to understand them- then get to be able to write "a feasible story" there are so many of the comments and conflicting reports as I have found--written by--**so called "experts"** on life and deaths of aboriginals in "massacres by The British" etc. I am trying to then advise readers here-- what I have found and-- what I think really happened--or— Did not happen.! Then I will say what I believe 'should' be done from here—it's easy to 'see' where we are going—but herein I will say--what I think **"the aboriginal race"** should do- and within these pages- I will endeavour to critique my research and findings--to explain why I say to all "activists"- Wake up.! What you are doing is **Not Helping**--you are creating--**a great Big divide in our population** where I say-- we should be as- One nation- **One Australia.!**

So- **what I am saying is that** "the First fleet"- **The British- Came here in peace**--to build a colony--to house convicts. They didn't bring troops or soldiers- bombs or big guns— they **did not** come to kill "the natives"—how often do we need to say this—because it should be "Obvious" to all-- That when Captain Phillip found such Primitive people who would have been "easy pickings"-- for another nation—Hey- guns- bombs- grenades- planes- against- the natives- with-- spears and boomerangs—**Aww cum on.?**

The Author — cont.

YES — I am The author--who left Tech. School at age 14- to be a carpenter- at 15- I built 1st Country house for neighbour. At 17 — was A Builder-towing tools in a box- on wheels- behind My pushbike — I built 9 houses — incl. one for my parents. At 19- doing national army service- was therein appointed The Builder to up-grade Army training circuit at Pucka Victoria. Then married with 3 children-to work for 'pa-in law'- a country bookmaker - learnt win% of TB racing and created <u>a bet plan</u>- to win each week. Later- joined EB sales in Bendigo- then transferred to Sydney- in NSW- where I Learnt the EB sales presentation — was a top Australasian salesman- then sales trainer- *experience that money can't buy--* To also win at weekend Races- to pay Our extra rent for 2 years. To move-to Melbourne where we had 3 family retail Shops--<u>Ever *'environment'* conscious</u>- I/Kev **won A 'Special' commendation** in 1985 **Energy Awards- on Neutral Carbon emissions-**A story in a book soon.! In 1995- Bought 3 mares- Raced with poor trainers. Bought 200 Acres, then over next 5 Years - bred Own 33 TB horses, Did bet/win at races to pay costs of 2 mortgages, 2 vehicle leases, stallion fees, vet fees, feed, Care for up to 36 horses- Trainer fees to race some. Kev did win $$s every week- **for 5 years**- to pay Costs- till in 2000- HIH Ins. Coy. Collapse- kills builder trade stops my kitchen sales income--Then A Bad Drought hit--eventually leading to Loss of stud farm and the horses. A long story- all about "Kevs Farm and Horses".

IN 2013 I/Kev became 'The Pioneer' of <u>*internet computer punt*</u> **To Win and pay-out $2.5million** to 70 sm. investors- I/*Kev tells* the story of <u>*other side to Gamble- called Punting*</u> in:-- **Need Money-'Kev's what if book'**- incl. 'help' for 'Problem gamblers'- It also tells of My Breakdown from — A Serious harass campaign-from A Guy- I did Treble his $$$ in a year.

THEN In- 2015- We did A Tour of Europe- London- saw the Palace- changing of the guards- Wimbledon- Rome- Vatican city- the Colosseum- Florence- Venice- where Casanova the world's greatest lover- was Locked in the Piombi-prison- HE became 'Inspiration for Kev's Stories of Love Books- On to Italy- Tirano- the Bernina express train over Alps to Switzerland- Zurich- Paris- the Opera house- Eiffel tower- Louvre- visited 'Henry V111' Church Ruins- and climbed the dome at St Pauls Cathedral--a fantastic Planes, Trains, an Automobiles- travel phenomena- gaining a great wealth of experience and knowledge which has become a background for a renowned international best-selling author of thrilling and captivating books- travel- Real life experiences- where Kevs 'Love' Books inspired by parts of Casanovas 'life'. Are 'stories of love'- which are 'different'- as Kev writes of how Casanova- was the first to commence-'the women's liberation" movement. Then also--Suspense and mystery robbery novels- which are sure to keep readers fully engaged and on edge of their seat- giving more from an assured multi-award-winning type author who already has achieved several accolades — from a lifetime of sports till settling into play squash- from local competition to Melbourne Masters-defeating 5 world master title holders- Kev's bet/win experience has been literally on all racetracks in Australia- earlier book story characters often being described as "intricate and brilliant" and his stories of love are totally "different"- assured of unforgettable reading enjoyment. So--those who seek a 'different' writer who has 'been there- done that'- one who writes unique-thrilling books with a wide range of genre- as won't disappoint. Author 'aussiekevG.'-- is the answer-- and **you will want-- Kev's books--** in front Row of your bookshelves too.!

The list of **'Kev's books'** can be found on page 297 herein.

Now--after *"the Personal plug"*-- here with this story--
the reason why--my research- did not--include talking to any aboriginal "<u>truth telling</u> elders" to create--this story — if its not already obvious — it will become obvious as we go along. But — before I began there were questions that I wanted to ask **Should I first** say *thanks to the aboriginal people-* who most pay homage to in their web pages.? Or what is one <u>expected to do- or say</u>--particularly for myself who has read about the *"mungo lady and mungo man"* --who experts said died here **62,000 years ago-** when aboriginals have, for <u>all of my life</u>- claimed to have been here for **55,000 years** — Saying that they were "**the Original"** owners of this land — they have always said that.! But then the powers that be- amended the '**mungo'** date- <u>it didn't suit</u>- they just wrote "the experts" off- as- they had made a **big** mistake.!?
But then — IT has all been a big mistake- because here now-- I learn that **"the mungo's"** have been known to aboriginals like — forever.? *I am yet confused--*
Like how could all of that happen — and we not know about it.?

<u>Even more so</u> — **now very** confused--with <u>my Own History</u>-- as I had recently read in an *"official visitor guide"*--created to 'Celebrate' 150 years of the Bendigo Easter fair- my home-town- in Victoria Australia--where my family have attended the Easter Parade for all of those years — myself--for at least a third of them-- now I see is featuring "dai-gum loon"-- the new Chinese dragon.! And- Bendigo is also where-in-the 50's- as a builder-at age 17- <u>To iterate</u>--I built 9 houses. I also Rode in the "Easter mile" Bike race-- to finish 4th — Close-- but No cigar.! The race that is still being run. **Well-- yes- all interesting stuff — but It was** <u>not until</u> I read- the **official visitor-guide book** –and I **learnt** that-- I was 'supposedly' born- reared- lived- Then married- to rear our 3 children in part of Australia — which the booklet now says —

The "Original" owners--say was *"a part of the Kulin nation"* where *"the dja-dja wurrung and Taungurung people"* were clans. And both were names as I- nor my folks- nor their parents- would never have heard of--which the 2022 guide says are 5 districts of communities closely related — now referred to as south-central Victoria- just **so amazing**--and all these years-- I thought I had lived in Central Victoria.! And none of my older family- several who lived to be 100+ in last two generations — nor I think- did the aboriginal boy- in my State school grade- we affectionately called "Grumpy"- of whom I had befriended. He rarely wore shoes or boots as the rest of us--I gave "Grumpy" a pair of my shoes at one stage- I recall he mostly wore them on the wet days- he was a character- on "show-n tell" days- he'd bring a snake -lizard- or spider-- I believe back then--even "Grumpy" would not have known- he was part of "the Kulin nation"-or even know what 'Kulin' meant- it wasn't discussed at school — not by 'Grumpy' nor by- our teachers (could be in future-who knows.)
All of which is totally amazing to be told this now in 2022. And-- to learn-- many of 'the old places' we knew- Eg:-- Sat. Nights (after we had 'set' our rabbit traps)--we'd go to the movies- at the Town Hall — which is now called as-- the "Star Cinema" and I guess that "Grumpy" wouldn't know-the Old Jail-- is now called the "Ulumbarra theatre" — or that here on the brochure-"the Djaara" and "Yorta-yorta"- people show *"a cultural Flower"* introducing it as an old *"aboriginal symbol of healing and of coming together"*-it's an-- Illuminated mural of--which they say is "a flower"- alas-- to me the picture looks nothing like a flower and — Surely- Not 'a flower' I doubt--if Grumpy ever knew of- as it is now 'created' by a modern-day aboriginal "artist" with-- Obvious- super imaginative-vision- to be able to create this most un-like "image" of- "A Flower"- except the "Flower"--

That is firmly ingrained-- in this artist's- own mind.!
I note:--there was no school education to tell much of our history" without favouring whites or blacks — I say--there should be a combined history--for 'future students' but — **NOT** as planned of aboriginal *"made-up"* **massacre** stories — **and the crap- as is b**eing proposed — to be using famed "historical writers details from books written by Milliss- Reynolds and others--and so-- my task herein will involve — to explain and demonstrate to readers —

How the "Furphies" - such as *'not being the Original owners'* and having *"the worst massacre in aboriginal history at Waterloo creek--when there was* No massacre — and--
> the soldiers who **massacred** 60+ at "Coniston -when-- there were No soldiers--

*This Myth-**would have been** **created** **by totally** un-trained- and non- schooled- un-educated elder aboriginals way back in 1800's when they also introduced- an incredible method of how they could be passing "messages" or instructions to younger generations via their "dream-time stories" — which- is actually using *'brainwashing'* techniques- to guide and control their people--which is quite unique and they have been doing this-- ever since the 1800's- with their 'Stories'. Those "Elders"-- who knew nothing of EB (encyclopaedia Britannica) even 100+ years ago- where they could not read nor write English-- to establish this mechanism — then to continually use it — to promote their "made-up stories" — Where their younger generations-- **sadly** grew up **believing- And trus**ting in their "dream-time stories" Is so fascinating.! As also hard to understand their people grew up believing -- And incredibly accepting-- without ever asking any questions-and The Elders- have achieved this-- right through To now in 2023--as they did not tell their kin — it was the format known as "brainwashing".

They Did not tell us of **'the mungo's"**- until-- 'the experts' tests--found the mungo's died here 62,000 years ago. I have done much research- kept looking for facts — only to learn — that their belief in this system is so strong — their generations of today-will not believe what anyone- other than "their truth teller elders" do tell them — as they continue to do this- without question.?
And — it is strange how things happen — because even just today — as I am writing this — I read someone had said that — *"learning – is something that no one can take away from you"* – and this so represents my situation as I am writing about here today — because everything that their "elders" have told these young aboriginals — everything they 'learnt' from the "elders' be it- true or false-
No way will they allow us- even myself to take that away from them — to change or try to be convincing them — that they have been 'fed false stories" — no way — because IF their "elders" told them-that's enough we know it is true.!
Even though my logic says otherwise — it will not matter — they will not believe me.!
But there is so much more to learn- and few genuine "Facts". To go/or build on--so then — I asked google- who was in Australia before the aboriginals —
Because —
I had read — *aunty val. Coombs,* A *Quandamooka Elder- in 2012- say:- white fellas like theorising we come from somewhere else – other than Australia to lessen our connection to country- we are from here--our knowledge of our history is embedded in our blood and our country. Whitefellas knowledge of our history only good as their technology. Aboriginal people are known to have occupied-- Mainland Australia for at least* **65,000 years**- *It's widely accepted this predates human settlement of Europe and the Americas.*

I note:--**aunty Val-** contradicts her 'Elders' in this **comment She made in 2012--** when aboriginals- right up till 2021-- Claimed to be *'Original'* owners from **55,000** years ago— Till the discovery of **"mungo lady" in 1967**— then **to find "mungo man"** in 1974. Which were both literally *"swept under the carpet"*-put away in a University vault--when "**experts" said they died here 62,000 years ago** which "the powers that be" said that's Not Convenient-- we should not believe that !
Here:--methinks *aunty Val-* is "a smart cookie" and she did already know of **"the mungo's"**— she had just tried to create an edge of **7,000** years to boost the *"Original"* 'status' for the Aboriginals-- as being 'the Owners'.
But then--suddenly later in 2021 it was **So confusing--**when came **"the shocker"**— **as** the experts—after "technology" did the DNA tests- **to prove** the mungo's HAD Died here 62,000 Years ago and DNA- was not same as aboriginal DNA.!
Then-- almost as if-- "someone was **reading my notes"** -- Co-incidently a main aboriginal web-site—then ***deleted*** its reference to **"the massacre** at waterloo creek" from its page.?
I wonder why.?
Well -because sadly as I see it the whole aboriginals belief-- their whole lives- has been built on or around a total of—on--going myriad of these **"Furphies"** and "made-up" stories - which generation-- after generation has been led to believe— It was True—when IT was all just-- **Crap**-.!
Ironically- I found- *that it began* **way** back in Capt. Phillip's Term when "the elders" used the death of **Pemulwuy's wife** and child- who died- from complications in childbirth— But—"those elders" took advantage of the situation and they Openly blamed Capt. Phillip-for their death- sending their "messages"- saying they were **"killed by The British"**—

So right from there--they have been constantly 'Feeding' similar type of 'stories' — to their Kin--
Sending "*made-up* stories "to their kin-- so close to blatant-- un-truths--inferring 'their' messages--were always true.?
Allowing Their Kin to "Believe" that they were True.!

Continuing with this form of *"brainwashing"*- as they have been using ever since —

To the point that now — my research has found that--

None really do know-- **what is right** — and —

what is wrong — and where today —

Because They only know what "Their Elders" have Told them--

SO--None can be sure —
 IF-- in fact —
  whatever they 'Thought' they knew--

  was EVER likely to be- True.?

The Power of —
"dream time stories"
repetition- repetition- repetition-

So Yes--I can *personally* relate to use *of* "brainwashing"- where I tell **another of my True Stories**--which I ask my reader to please remember-- because it also is True- and this Could easily be You — my Reader:--
Ok-some years ago, 'our family Kitchen Coy.'- contracted to make a new "Architect designed" kitchen--and install it-- for A Builder *(we had done hundreds of kitchens and bathrooms etc)*- Here we found the architect- had made a mistake--his Plan-- wouldn't fit. Frid. pm- Builder rushed to our showroom- Asks me to fix it — said he had authority--so we can re-make these Cabinets to fit--*I said we would do alters at cost--**to help him-*** *which we did. But--as a fool--I believed him--didn't even ask him to **sign an "amendment form"**.* Later then at Install the Architect- had not approved "the changes"- so he refused to accept the kitchen-because it then would *not be* 'His kitchen' (which wouldn't fit). **The reality which is relevant here is:—** The Builder I made the alters for- knew He was Wrong-- had left me and told his legal and his wife *"a made-up story"*--so as to not look like He was the one who had made a mistake- He then repeated that **"made-up story"** to many people-- so many times — he'd convinced himself-- had **'brainwashed'** his wife- and his legal- and all those around him- to Believe that it was true, and--finally He-his wife and all DID **believe it was true.!** **In court- on day one--**we could not get him to admit- nor to accept--that he had made this story up-- it was not at all how it had happened. But *I had no proof* — and now-- Three months later-- He is totally convinced that His story - HIS *"Made-Up"* Story was the truth — As He then —

108

Swore On The Bible.! **So- right there--**I stopped Our proceedings — Yes- we are 100% right. But I knew NO- we couldn't win.! So- I did "A Deal" and — I bought Our kitchen back from him. Then the Architect- had someone else--make a brand "New" Kitchen --*Exactly the same as our kitchen*-- the one we made after we fixed His Errors- But here *you see*- This kitchen was NOW-- **The Architects — "Own Design".!?**

The moral **of this experience here being —** I see many of these highly titled historians who are "writing aboriginal history" with "*imagination and narration*"--**not facts, and-- Sadly** the many un-suspecting young aboriginals- and the Governments--**don't understand or accept** that these **are just "made-up" stories** as over and over--they continually are being **brainwashed** each time they read this Rubbish.! Yes**- I have had very — very-- costly Personal experience-- I "Did A Deal"** because--I had already learnt of the huge Power of "Brainwashing" in 'EB'(encyclopaedia Britannica.) When I Trained to learn their sales pitch/Presentation — then was 'A Trainer' of New EB Recruits- at Wollongong nsw. **So HERE- I feel totally qualified-- to write this story--** because the "aboriginal story"--*as I see it*-- IS of "the elders using their *brainwashing* techniques** to guide and control both *"the direction" and 'thinking"* of the whole aboriginal race - from 230+ years ago- right to here — today- **and-- I do emphasise--**I am one of *"a few--still alive"*- at least in Australia--who could have been trained by and have Sold many products using The EB sales training program —

As was used Prior to computers and the internet.!
This "**brainwashing**" technique- I still use constantly — to help myself and try to help others today. So- what I see here-- is what has been used by the "truth telling" aboriginal Elders--since Forever--**First to create**--*then to* foster — *the world's greatest* "Furphy" ever seen-- To create "a Furphy" which has caused really tremendous "ripple effects" year in and year out — over more than 200+ years. I Do understand- because with 'EB'--I was one of the Top salespeople and then have also trained- many other 'sales staff and groups' and private minds- just as here with the 'elders'-who have- right to today- been using their own "**brainwashing**"-- as here I can see — that literally 'forever'-- this information- has been fed to all the younger generations of aboriginals, who have **No Idea- that** their "trusted elders" really have been "*brainwashing*" them- and they would not believe- that most of their history stories of Their Families — they have heard of-- or read- and believed-- have mostly just been- The "Elders" Own **Made-up stories**.!
So here then:- when looking at writing this story--I become- like a guy who has 'found' a million piece--jigsaw puzzle- and I am trying to complete it — to put it all together-- when so many pieces have been- swapped- twisted- altered or moved around so much they just won't--fit.!
So-what to do.? My task here-- is not to try to discover how many were killed or **if--** they were killed — although actually- My-- research does 'contradict' — totally dis-regards- for--

Example--**Ms Ryan's** *'massacres map'* where- I see massacres are-'Found' by some kind of her "magic formulas"--or her extra-ordinary vision—but her 'map' remains valid- **ONLY-- Because** No one has **ever challenged** her 'findings'--and yes- I believe that The Government even issued 'subsidies' to Help produce this <u>'Crap'</u>—but **its valid because** No One did ever question <u>her credibility</u>—No One ever asks things like:- -Exactly- where were they massacred- Who Killed them- and- How—Then <u>what happened to the bodies</u> or—Do we have the body bones.? Surely - one would think- that whoever "approved" The $$ Subsidies to produce this "massacres map"- would say like—We want to SEE Bodies- we want Details.? Like <u>where are All of the bodies.?</u> There simply CAN'T be 1,000s **"massacred"** and there be NO bodies **ever found-- that's <u>Totally Illogical</u>—It's just not possible**.!

Yet—it appears The Govt. Member who Approved some Subsidy here--Did not Ask for these Things--and the highly titled and so respected professor continues to flaunt her 'massacre' claims -which to me **is totally un-believable-** that 'they' did approve such $$ subsidy and not ask <u>**where are the bodies.?**</u> To Me-- It surely sounds as if—**'the approver'-- was also an aboriginal.!** Now with THIS **"<u>brainwashing</u>"**— I Explain "The difference"--<u>between</u> All of the aboriginals— Myself and my Fellow Sales Trainees IS *<u>simply that</u>*. **We all did know- <u>We Volunteered</u> our minds to be trained** to be **"brainwashed"-- As Part of** learning 'the EB sales pitch'-- So We Did **know-- Why** we were being "<u>brainwashed</u>".? But here 'the aboriginals' **<u>Do Not know</u>**- and they did NOT--

Volunteer to be brainwashed--yet- their "elders" have been- and still are "brainwashing" them — **'brainwashing'** their Own kin — even when to learn they have lied to them for years and If **the "mungo'" lie-** *had not been made public — then their kin still **would not have been told**.!* And you my reader would not have known WHY — We now call aboriginals just as "the Custodians" of this land--**you- would not have-- believed Me--when I said**--the entire race has been 'Used'-- *'brainwashed'* and *'manipulated'* as well as **Our governments** and our entire Australian population- None did know they were ALL being misled — being totally *misled* by these-- "*truth teller*" aboriginal "elders"-- for 230+ yrs.

BUT again- came Confusion as:--First **Proven** by in 2021 the revelation of **the "mungo's' as** being found to have died here **62,000** years ago- and the **DNA** was not aboriginal--**Wow-- **That was-- Oh boy — what "*a real bummer*"- then suddenly and with No Notice- they are not now--**the Original** owners at all — and are just to be called as "*the Custodians*" of the land.? And since then- ALL Businesses have acknowledged that — And AS 'Elders' since- have performed "Welcome To Country" Smoke Ceremonies — They have Done so AS-- "*The Custodians* of The Land" — But then as 'the other 96.7% 'of the Population had begun to Accept this Change- IN 2023 Others' as The PM aided by Aboriginal "Activists" suddenly are all Gung Ho-Leading The Charge to have "A Voice" In Parliament acting on behalf **"The FIRST NATIONS People"** and Then--The Prime Minister had Turned everything Around — again — Because to Advocate- HIS "Voice" To be--

Heard On behalf **"First Nations People"** — Here HE has turned this problem area Upside-Down once again-and again I Ask — DOES ANYONE Really Know what Has Happened to "The Mungo" Theory.?

And as we are Voting on A Voice for "First Nations People"- Why are "The Elders" still being Called ***"The Custodians"*** *Of This Land — and Not "Original Owners".?* And yet--at the same time Our PM IS Pushing For 'A Voice' for The FIRST Nations People- of 65,000 Years Ownership.? .

The aboriginal websites say we use:-

'the power of <u>*truth-telling*</u> to realise change'.

But — even when we do know <u>the truth</u> —

the "real truth" — which — is not--

No--it's not as aboriginals intended us to know--

But — they continue on as **"First Nations People".?**

NOW--<u>*IF I wasn't The Author here*</u> —

I would be inclined to **"Give Up".!**

<u>**BUT Instead**</u> — here now —

To better Help Readers understand what I am talking about- I will now explain **"The Game"** We Teens played at some of our Parties- way back in My Younger Days--

We Didn't Have Computers- I Phones -Game Boys or Mobile Phones — SO instead — We played 'Games'- such as This — At Parties-- Just for Harmless Fun — for laughs: —

We called it- **"Pass it on"** — I present IT to give <u>*An Example*</u> of how the 'Elder Aboriginals' made up ***Stories*** will surely-

113

"Change" as they are passed on.? Just as we would pass on- "A Story"- as eg:-- about "Mary".? To **demonstrate**-- **The Game we teens played many years Ago-** For--a laugh - at parties, where say 12 people would line up-- we would write- a simple message on a pad- as eg:—
To say:-- *Mary has a friend--they want to get married and have kids and to travel one day."* —

We would then- *whisper* This message to a person — like the 1st in line and softly say:--***Pass it on*** —
Pass it on **verbally**- softly- to next IN Line — then 10 -or 12 friends in turn--would then whisper 'the message' — and say-
 "Pass it on"--
Then--at the end — after each one had **"Passed it on"** —
Normally each did either add a little-- or changed it a little But then **The last in line**- would Write 'The Message Down'-

the end result We would find--could be something as eg:--

Mary- has 5-6 kids — the guy wouldn't marry her- and she hopes to move away — to get away from him-- to start a new life--with her family--somewhere else — overseas in future.!

This is what happened **back then** — at Our Parties and I say-- **LOGICALLY**--This IS what has been happening with The Aboriginals--AS **there**--each one adds their 'take'--onto "the Elders" story-- it gets worse/or becomes different-- as it is passed on —

Till eventually: *they lose all semblance of the "Original" message.!* Then--**No one knows what/or- who- was right or wrong**- SAME as at Our Parties--about — "Mary" .!

I Say--THIS IS EXACTLY--
What has been happening with the "Elders stories" here--- with the young aboriginals — and could my Reader Imagine How much those "Stories" would have 'Changed'--Time and time again-- over some 200+ Years.?
Yes — I find — it is — **EXACTLY** — the case here — like to just imagine back say 200 years ago when my great- great- Great- Great- great- great Grand Father —
May have said--
"would you please be careful — Don't Go near 'The Settlers' — Be Sure to Tell your Friends too.!" —

To Say This to Two youngsters- who were there- "Play-fighting" happily together' —
Imagine then — what likely could have happened Next —
Then--when "Activists" Passed IT On- 200 Years later —
It's Not hard to--Imagine what "aboriginal activists" Said-- or Did--when They heard about this.?

Oh Sweet-- "Mary"--

Who knows-By Now--

SHE--Likely would have had--
    Some 20 Husbands and 60+ Children.?
       Kev.

The 1942 Darwin war .?.

SO-- why-- do we NOT have —

A "Special" Darwin war day to celebrate.?

Why do they waste everyone's time, money-- and "trust"-- with "the massacre" at waterloo creek —
that never did happen--
Why.?
Yes--Why do we NOT have--

A "Special"-
Darwin war day--
for All Australians to celebrate.?

To give thanks to those brave people...
To those Brave "Fighters"--One and all--

Who stopped *the Japanese army--*
From being the Last Owners of this land.?
I ask--
Why do we not have A "Special" —

Darwin war day...
For ALL Australians to celebrate.?

THIS—WAS The Japanese Invasion--
Of Darwin--IN 1942

Why Do we Not have A Darwin war day
Australia Wide--why not.?

A "Special"-
Darwin war day--
for All Australians to celebrate.?

To give thanks to those brave people…
To those Brave "Fighters"--One and all--

Who stopped *the Japanese army*--
From being the Last Owners of this land.?
I ask--
Why do we not have A **"Special"** —

Darwin war day…
For ALL Australians to celebrate.?

To digress for a moment — *To return to "Aboriginal Deaths"* — *BY Contrast: With* The DARWIN War — *where we have ALL Bodies Accounted for — Alive and Killed*--**ALL On RECORD--** It is incredible to see The Number of FALSE Reports — as I did Find IN the compound total of all the massacre sites I have just browsed through on the Internet — there are hundreds of thousands of "Claimed" massacred bodies--everywhere — On The Net--but the bodies have all somehow just gone and "*disappeared*" -- it appears as if by "Black magic".
Simple answer--**my logic says-** because the bodies were never there in the first place:--to be found or to disappear-- as these were all "*made-up stories*"--*as* the elders continued to use to fill the young heads with — as they were creating Angst and-- Vitriol against "the first fleet" — 'The Invaders' and their descendants.! Ironically — their young people *all did believe* them- no matter the logic- no- matter how impossible the story- or The Claim--they *all believed* these were *true — because* "they wanted to believe these *made-up stories*- from their "*truth teller*" elders were ALL really true.! Same as the profit seeking writers when they introduced- **'Genocide'** and **'Frontier wars'--**which no one had heard of b*efore these* sensationalist writers *introduced it*- **in their books** -when **The Writers** wrote it as "a gimmick — A Hook"- to better help Sell their books and videos etc. Wikipedia defines these as:-- genocide is the deliberate and systematic destruction, in whole or in part, of an ethnic, racial, religious, or national group. The term was first coined in 1944. (In Books.?)
Frontier wars--the Australian frontier wars were the violent

conflicts between indigenous Australians and primarily British settlers during the colonisation of Australia. FALSE Reports say-- *The first conflict took place several months after* the landing of the first fleet in January 1788, and the last frontier Conflicts occurred in the early 20th century, with some occurring as late as 1934. Where An estimated minimum of **100,000** indigenous Native Australians and 2,000-2,500 settlers died in the conflicts. The 'Conflicts' occurred in a number of locations across Australia... (Un-Proven 'Locations'.)
I note:-- *'anyone can create their own entries on these Information Platforms'- with regards- 'frontier wars'- the notations obviously were made by aboriginal "activists" - after 2010- on arrival of-- "the internet In Australia"* — *and they directly* contradict *daily Entries in* the journals *made by Captain Phillips & Co-*
But — again- HERE on Wikipedia- **This 'Activist' has jumped** from "A Historical Writers 20,000" Now Up to 100,000 Of The Aboriginal/Native Australians and 2,000-2,500 settlers died IN 'Conflicts' — BUT here again — They Found NO Bodies — nor Body Bones either-- And there is no mention--NO reports of where any of those dead bodies were buried- or- of what did happen to the Bodies or Body Bones.?
AND I can't forget that 'Windschuttle wrote' — It was likely that the Deaths of Whites — by far Outnumbered those of Blacks.?
But here-- even though we now know these were- **NOT true** IT is amazing- how they continue to "attack"--the rest of the population"--saying we should *"tell the truth"*- because they believe "their elders" without any question- and these type of reports are what 'they' are including within **'Our History'** which is to be presented to Our children at schools — Remembering--Ironically — this is being created by the 3.3%

Of Aboriginals- to be presented to 96.7% of Other children.? AND--As I guess- to be *paid for- by Australian Govt – supported by the ABC.* Yes--I am continually amazed to learn, how so much of the aboriginal "history" was being created from '*made-up*' **Crap** Stories--which also came from another Elder' "*made-up* story".! Which Yes I can understand- how IT all happened — Because as I said--I am one of the old sales people who trained and live with **'*power of brainwashing*'** So here I believe that not one of 'the experts' — or 'historical writers'-ABC- SBS--TV producers- least of all--none of '*the truth teller*' elders- Could stand in front of us today to say they **honestly Do** know exactly what happened way back there in colonisation of Australia

Not one of these people-- nor anyone else today — could ever be able to do that- simply because- it is not possible that anyone alive today- could have been there in 1788 or in 1838.! Yet--in the early years- there are journals as were written like- Daily by Captain Phillip and crew — many were published later in UK — Some of which I did peruse

But most of the aboriginal historical writers-- didn't use this Material - and instead-- wrote their own versions- wrote their own ideas-- and their extensions of "the Elders stories"- some 185+ years later- most not reading or ever accepting that 'The Journals' were in fact accurate —

But- their own "*made-up* stories" grew from early 1900's and then "blossomed" from 2010--when they found **'the internet'**-which means literally everything- as each person--

Black or White – Do <u>think</u>- that they know-- about what 'happened' within colonisation — it is just *"their opinion"*- based upon — *"someone else's" opinion*-- formed — from an elders *"<u>made-up</u> story'*-which was-another version of a story of what someone else had already written — at least 3 Times. **So — I write to say** "Wake up" **Australia — because it's time to Say — and Do something — TIME To Change Tact.!** I ask to be excused for referring to "them and us" but within this story that is really just an extension of what aboriginal-- "Activists" seem intent upon creating today — to separate "them & us"--and I want to try to *"turn that around"*- but no This is not an easy book to write — on this subject-- because on the one side — I must "<u>take my hat off</u>" to all those who have Spent years gaining- an education- Yes- <u>obviously</u> paid for by The Govt. They do totally disregard and do wish to-- Be rid of--and of course they could not have gained such education -without help *from "descendants of the First fleet"*-- But also Let's NOT Forget — THEY likely would Not BE Here **IF it wasn't for The Descendants of The First Fleet-** **WHO Fought to SAVE Them** — from **The Japanese Army** — Yet it-- seems they gain "$$ subsidies" from The Govt.-- who they totally disregard and disrespect--and they prosper by using every possible government Fund or facility- subsidy- as has ever been available- to help them- To Protest. Yes- <u>it is</u>-- so really <u>weird</u>- because *on the one hand*--**Capt. Phillip**- *would have been **<u>so pleased</u>** to see these aboriginals become so well educated — to have studied to attain their titles — to be so highly regarded — and yet — <u>He would also be so sad</u>*-- that they are using-

124

This education-- trying to destroy the structure that 'the British' have worked so hard- and fought to create for them -- and to also help- the 96.7% of all other Australians.

Yet today — the 3.3% use--all of the modern IT- computers- TV- Govt. Funded ABC- as they and their families Live in top quality housing- either supplied by Govt. Or paid for--by their- higher than normal salaries and subsidies. All as Capt. Phillip-- not in so many words-- but had told them that this was what he had wanted <u>for them</u>. Yet--he would not have meant that this transition was to literally divide them into Two groups within their own people- to have the bottom half yet live in humpies 230+ years later--as Some use the education to also create and extend-"<u>the great divide</u>"- between whites and coloured--where the effects of this Now- has most "activists" carrying on as total deceitful protesting- Taking part in any type of movement as are intent on trying to destroy the govt — and the people <u>as they are being paid by</u> and/or- likely also funded by a govt. Subsidy.

All of which I really do have trouble getting my head around- like, its- 235 years since Captain Phillip landed in Botany Bay to build a colony to house the overflow of-- British convicts-- mostly guilty of crimes as steal a loaf of bread or similar- which of course <u>was why</u> the First fleet did not-- Include Soldiers and lots of guns and why--totally contrary-- to as the "activist's" would have us believe- as one said--<u>I reiterate</u>--*there was armed conflict- from day one — we fought them then and we still fight them now".?* Where- I point out-- this statement <u>Totally</u> contradicts Capt. Phillips--

Journals which reported, that on landing-- *To re-iterate:--*
"they had exchanged trinkets — danced & sang with the natives
and some elders had dinner with Capt. Phillips on board the ship.?
Later he wrote that just-- 4 natives had died/killed, and that
many of his convicts had also died of illness- some were
killed by the natives. I Say that figure- was pre-start of
<u>Pemulwuy's</u> rebellious 3 year reign of destruction- at The
Colony — yet the activists say these things that are *totally in-*
*correct- b*ut somehow They find ways to have them printed
in our Newspapers--maybe installed on web pages or
internet-- where they are read <u>and believed</u> by thousands of
people- **and because none ever** "challenged" the statement
or--order to re-print or "re-call" etc   So then-- IT becomes--
<u>A Fact.?</u> Just as none ever queried how it could be published
"un-checked" in a Daily Newspaper so- when-- The younger
aboriginals read IT — they naturally <u>believe it is true</u>.?
Same as hundreds of entries I found--ALL Claiming to have
'Found' Hundreds or Thousands as were Massacred--Yet
None of those hundreds of Claims did mention — where
there were bodies found--yet — each were Sure--that great--
Numbers had been Massacred- just as Ms Ryan's "massacre
map"- of 174 massacre sites "found" — but yet No bodies or--
Body bones- were 'found' by The Expert Ms Ryan's team.!
And all of this — after they have gained an education — Paid
for by those as they "Fight" to be rid of today — and Who
they gain "subsidies" from — To Pay to create this Rubbish.!
So yes I see younger generations were ever "brainwashed"
by the Elder "activists" as they do--pass their bias —

"Made-up stories" on- as "facts"-plus- as each "elder" sent their version of a story--they add a little- and it grows worse-- as they pass on their versions of the earlier elders-"*made-up stories*" — then the lop-sided' activists- all jump on any "new thing as stated" no matter how ridiculous the claim- but as it came from <u>truth-teller</u> Elders- they then believe-that it must be true--**It is incredible–**how young aboriginals have totally believed and- for anyone to <u>not believe this,</u> then--well- it is as activist-*"truth teller"* writer *"Professor Chelsea Watego"* bond says in Her book-- **For Me-- 'a white'**- to write as herein-- Then- I am but- <u>in her view</u> *"one of the fictions of white folk and their fanciful psychological journeys"*--<u>in laymen speak</u> — this means-- herein- <u>I do my Own research</u> don't listen to/or Study- The **Rubbish** most of the aboriginal activist writers as 'Ms Watego'--have "force fed" the country with- for all-- Of our lives--which they all write as being 'Facts'- yet- they have- just learnt it from *their <u>truth telling</u> "elders"*-- likely in *"dream time stories"*- and so- **"the Porkies"** keep growing.! Yet to the younger aboriginals--whatever it be- if their-- "<u>Truth telling elders</u>" said it-- Then it must be true and as-- 'Ms Watego'- <u>infers</u> *That if We the other 96.7% of the population* <u>**don't believe**</u> *what they/she says — then it is- WE- who are either "racist' or **on** "fanciful psychological journeys"- and ARE part of "creating" the divide in our population-* because We don't Accept what they/she says Is True-- Yet they only know that-'its' True—because their "Elders" told them it was True as-- Eg:-- there were up to 1,000 massacred- their elders said- but yet No bodies are found—But <u>it's True</u>.!

Because "The Elders" Told us so.? Which I say is totally unbelievable and way beyond all normal logic- which is the reason why--no way-- I will talk to any of "the elders" to gain their version-to help me write this My book --as it seems mostly the historical writers have tended to have done, in the past and-- then have written "their own versions" of what "the *truth teller* elders" had said-like *300 to 1,000 massacred at Waterloo creek.? When only 10-12 were Shot and 7 (seven) others were killed by Major Nunn's group.* Now — the difference with the high educated professor Ms Chelsea Watego (as I have Not met.) and myself IS that-- when I hear things such as that--I immediately will ask-- *how could that physically even be possible- as I can't imagine 300 to 1000 dead bodies--all lying in a very shallow-narrow creek — and No bodies or body bones--TO* ever be found*-* I can't imagine that — Because my simple logic says — it's not possible--no matter how they were buried — they would have been found — which to Me means IT could Not be True-- Whereas I Guess then--Ms Watego- would likely believe it-- *without question*- because she was told this by *'a trusted elder"- Then* She would surely 'Pass it on'--or maybe then Write of it in one of her Books- to also add her own 'take' — TO then Deride me as being *"one of the fictions of white folk and their fanciful psychological journeys"* Because **I would not believe** that Rubbish.! But then I have found their "Belief" is just so amazing. Yet there ARE Questions as Eg:- I recently read a report- as said stuff like *"people as very knowledgeable professor's- for example- successful in their own fields — when they extend into 'a second loop'" —*

"Their logic often is flawed- or goes astray".! <u>If to apply this logic here</u>—it could be as Ms Watego's quoted analysis of Me "a white"-could be something like "<u>self- analysis</u>".? Or again "the war strategy" which I referred to earlier-- *'attacking'* anyone who does not Agree with her comments.? <u>But say:- re. 300 to 1,000 bodies</u>- *IF we do consider* <u>*this was true*</u> then Seriously what did happen to all of those 300 to 1000 dead bodies.? No way 'the soldiers'(who weren't there.) would be 'detailed' to dig the holes to bury that many bodies Then if they burnt them—that would have taken ages—and there would still be some bones left-- to be found.? **So-- I wonder**—what then really did happen to those 300 to 1,000 bodies.? Because I say- *Even if it was true--that so many were to have been massacred*-That many bodies would be impossible to bury in such a Shallow Creek-- that later dried up—and still- None of those bodies- or body bones- to ever be found-- **Totally impossible.?** But to re-iterate-- I have found the real problem, has been--That no one has <u>ever challenged</u> such Ridiculous statements-So then being left un-challenged IT became "a fact" as *the "*<u>*truth teller*</u>*" elders--then passed on-- to their kin--*<u>*as being true*</u>.? The profit seeking writers wrote their versions of it- <u>added stuff</u>- like Milliss's *"to 300 were slaughtered—as another wrote to 20,000 aboriginals were slaughtered or massacred in British colonisation of Australia.?* I mean for the "dedicated activists" this kind of <u>rubbish'</u>--has been the stuff that they dwell on--Its the stuff that helps fire them up.! <u>Albeit- 'Keith Winspear'</u> did write that--*the historic writer "Reynolds"—had tallied up the Whites killed—multiplied it—*

129

And wrote the total up as being Total Aboriginals killed-BY whites.? *Later in the 2000's-then Professor Ryan created her "massacres map" but-again--she with all her titles- and skill- still did not* find any bodies *or body bones-- either.* So-in all--none of the people, the "experts" — the writers-- then with the hundreds of "massacre" entries on the net — not one- ever did show any evidence of what happened to those dead bodies — as 'they' claimed--were slaughtered or massacred by the "invaders"- None of these people — ever did find any of the purported slaughtered bodies of the "massacres" they "found".!

But- Who cares about proof- bodies- bones or "evidence".?

"NO--let's not spoil--a good story-- Hey".?

THE LANDING

To write any story about either the aboriginals or – Captain Phillip's landing in 1788- it must first be noted that Captain cook on his 'Endeavor'-- a purpose built Ship- did land 14 times- to 'charter' this land--Capt. Cook – raising-- The British flag- on this land in 1770 was –
Yes--for The British-and also-to ward off a likely "invasion" by China or **the Dutch**--China were known to have 'mapped' most coast lines of Australia – then known as "terra nullius"-meaning "land belonging to no-one"-as well- "the Dutch"- were already calling the land "new holland"- so in Capt. Cooks review- **'the act'** of "raising the British flag" – was to claim it as British – but to also be one of-- 'protecting' the country from others who could want to "take over" complete possession of all of the land.?

Capt. Cook raised the British flag in 1770.

In- recent times- google says:--<u>Alison page</u>--a Walbanga and Wadi- wadi person of the Yuin nation, grew up in the botany bay area- where- cook earlier stepped ashore.
She recently travelled the east coast speaking to indigenous people for a film about cook's voyage, told <u>from an aboriginal perspective</u>- and says-- *"in the lead up to this commemoration, we've only just started to hear the other side of the story, which is the story from the shore,"* Ms. Page said- *"i grew up thinking captain cook was **the bogeyman** and that he was responsible for the displacement of my people and our culture."* so--as we sift through ideas about who discovered Australia, Ms Page thinks we might find something unexpected in the commemoration of cook's voyage to Australia as <u>she says</u>-- *"it's interesting this word 'discovery', because I think we are going to go on a journey of discovery,"* she said. *"but that discovery doesn't speak to England's discovery of new lands, but actually Australia's discovery of its own Identity."*
I wonder--did Ms Page know-the truth.? was she warning of "<u>Mungo's</u>"--and *the real discovery- yet to come.?*

No--Cook didn't actually claim he had discovered Australia- but- **Capt. Cooks** <u>HMS Endeavour</u> **had** landed *14 times* on the east Australian coastline. One landing was in the waters of Botany bay. **He** wasn't the first Englishman to arrive here—William Dampier set foot on the peninsula <u>that now bears his name,</u> north of Broome, in 1688.
Captain cook named the land where he first raised the flag as **"new south wales"-- in an effort <u>to counter</u>** any China or Dutch interest in what they had long called "new holland."
It is interesting to note that 'Ms Page' says--
From her early days--she understood **captain cook was responsible** for--*"the displacement of my people and loss of our culture." —*

133

Obviously- it would appear that Ms. Page- was also **misled** by her "elders" — which has become "*a common thread*" within my aboriginal story.?
Re:--"*the displacement of my people and loss of our culture.*" — To research this- was not easy- as first-- the aboriginals were listed as people who move from place to place — Nomads-- where their houses were 'Humpies" — the men hunted for kangaroo- wallaby- etc for meat — women scavenged for berries-fruit-etc.

It was a surprise for them to learn- that the 'settlers' could grow cattle and wheat etc for flour and grow vegetables for eating and for cooking-- early days Capt. Phillip reported they did continue to hunt and fossick for their food — later then- the aboriginals did not move out to hunt and scavenge for meat & berries etc as —

Instead- rather than helping settlers to grow their food- It Appears- most found it easier to just take/steal food from the settlers. Which it appears was where much of the problems began.

So-- the meaning of this- and its effects as reported on many aboriginal web sites-- is difficult to find any more than each site talking about all of the 'things' as run around proving their existence of slaughter and massacres —

which my research shows most *likely did not happen* —

The journals say captain Phillip said the plan was to teach the natives how to produce a food chain — which is hard to relate to--because it seems that the aboriginals didn't want to Do this- Didn't want to co-operate- they didn't want to learn how to create a food chain.!

So- then the claim:--

> *"the displacement of my people and our culture--*
> is difficult to find answers to.?

Because:--the colony would have just used an area-- like one of our now small suburbs — when — there was so much land area available.!

And as 'Nomads' — Capt. Phillip and those to follow — surely would have expected the natives — to move out — or maybe to work around them — because — there was just so much land as was not being used--

The Australian land-
Is a very large area--the 6th largest country comprising 7.692024. Sq.klms

 I point out--in 1788--the 'British' settlers came-- wanting just a small area — of Botony bay / Sydney.- to build a colony. To house their convicts--

136

The Landing- in 1788 —
the First fleet ships sailing into 'botany bay'-

We come bearing gifts and not to use guns.

Other Opinions

Now--before I move on-- I want to 'touch on' what some *'others think'* and start with-- the reason behind all of the kafuffle about *"the mining company logo"* and in my view-- the "activists" behind misleading comments from "the reporters" (aboriginal) who jump on any opportunity that can help them 'to write a new story--to stretch or twist the things' to suit their own agendas.

So- for me-- when deciding to write this story--I have found that it's like we- my side of the community- live a progressive somewhat "normal life" — yet-- it seems "aboriginal people" from the esteemed Professors--down to those as still-- sit in Humpies — well- they don't appear to want to do the same.

Don't seem to want to ever **"call it a draw"** — constantly creating "activist" type actions — constantly **ignoring** that **"the Darwin war"**--**did actually happen**.!

They just won't see how that war and Aussies- Aboriginals and Allies **fighting together** has **changed everything**— Because fact is-- had The Allied army — *not been here to fight* -- **the Japanese off--t**he Japs-who were intent on **"Invading--and taking over"** this country — surely would have--

Massacred--The whole Aboriginal race.!

But the "activist" aboriginals- don't see that as being In any way--significant--as they continually mouth off about seeking "A Treaty"—

I ask — 'treaty' **for what**- "gifts or freebies" Land that *None now could survive on.?* Because everything aboriginals could need- **The Government** has since made available — and if they had saved money- if they would work- they can buy land-- same as any of us-- if we have deposits- work history — solid credit worthiness- enough income etc--same as it is for everyone.! If they want to mix in--they can--but because of "Activists" actions-- and 'Elders' dream time —

140

'Stories' with their false **brainwashing--I See** <u>they will never Mix In</u>--Most who already do draw pension or the dole — use it as a reason Not to work--to mainly buy smokes- alcohol- or- drugs with no future planning likely visible — because they don't want to plan--A Future — they don't seem to want to mix to join in--'the activists' have created a totally "anti-Australian Government" attitude — starting years ago- saying things as *"they didn't need to steal the children".!* And even recently — another talented young aboriginal girl--sang one of elder "archie Roach" songs about *"the children"* and how-- they were "Taken" — yet — the song did not tell **Why-- the children were "taken"- no--**they never say **Why--they** never admit to the reason being--that it was to get them away from family rape and violence- to be sure they were properly cared for and well educated —

Yet today <u>it seems</u> — **nothing has really changed**--as many of "the elders"--<u>it seems</u>--still rely on the young girls in their group/tribe/clan- for their sexual relief — It's like they are in some "time warp" from 230+ years ago — 'they' didn't want to 'co-operate' with captain Phillip way back then- when the British had laws to stop Rape and domestic violence--and 'the elders' then--didn't want to 'co-operate" nor do they want to co-operate today- and they appear to be still living just as their ancestors lived- and are doing- what it appears their "Elders" did-- back then-- and these people are in the same mode- except back there- they never had the dole or pension — and of course — back there they--couldn't "blame" the government — as they do today.!

So- this--My story- is also about--putting "myths" to rest, and trying to un-ravel--how it is that "activists" and others can make <u>totally Illogical</u> statements and accusations of atrocities- murders -massacres and the like — <u>Yet none can relate to a site</u> where bodies were "found"-

Except Waterloo Creek (7)-- **Myall creek (28) -a**nd one site in WA.(14)--to justify their—Wild Statements- or—To prove their people were <u>even</u> anywhere near those sites—as they claim.?
And--how they <u>do</u> <u>Not</u> agree that The Darwin war- in 1942-- WAS—Significant- to them.!
This is the issue I face-- in preparing this material.

Same as here I read "generation" reports as are written--so often without due diligence or caring about "facts" or to not include all of the story- <u>I refer to</u>--the recent comments as reported <u>the nasty words</u> "lang Hancock" supposedly said 40 years ago—and here *the aboriginal "activists" want his daughter Gina-- 40+ years later-- to say Sorry – or to declare that she didn't share her father's views.!* **Omg—**so these "activists" are so very concerned by some "nasty words" <u>mayb</u>e spoken 40 year ago. Yet—**"they" Can't relate** to the single important event that-- **could have wiped out their whole aboriginal race—**could have slaughtered them all. **I** <u>re-iterate:</u>-- Yes-- <u>the Darwin war</u>—in 1942 where aboriginals fought- side by side with descendants of "the first fleet"- to **Save Australia—to Save-- the whole Aboriginal Race—**and then **Japan** would have been--not <u>the</u> "<u>original</u>" owners--but-- *"the Last owners"* --of this land.! **Incredibly** "aboriginal activists" can relate to "nasty words" <u>mayb</u>e said to their "Elders" in 'the 80's'--Yet don't recall-- "the question" as drew 'the nasty words'--As--they and their "elders" **Conveniently** <u>don't remember</u>--The Darwin war **that saved-- their whole aboriginal race.?** And here today— they want to question a woman who has- Paid $millions to the aboriginals in royalties as she has spent many $millions-- to help young aboriginals—paid many $millions helping Australian Sports teams which include Aboriginals—and helped with many $millions in other areas-as well—

142

All of which these "activists" simply **_don't recall_** and just **disregard--**because it suits their agenda's.!
Here in the case of "nasty words"--**my guess is**—It could well have been related to--*how to control* **the huge problem-** known back then of--*in-breeding and sexual abuse of young aboriginals-- with the ritualistic and sexual practices on young girls as were "reportedly" so often carried on by "the elders" of each tribe or clan which has been said to be behind the often criticised "removal of young aboriginals"* from their parents by the Government—To Save those children.
Still decried by the "activists" who labelled it as-"_the stolen generation_"-but don't tell/admit Why-the children were "taken"-- they continue to blame the Govts- claiming there was _no reason_ *for the children to have been 'stolen'* even knowing the children had been removed to avoid them suffering at the hands of their own family or "elders"— which of course **"activists" to today--still strongly deny**.!
Yet—records show- that such sexual abuse does still occur—and Yes 'the governments'—I see--_from another direction_—could be partly to blame- as they did bring Rum (alcohol) here with 'the First fleet'- and from there it has appeared to become a part of aboriginal lifestyle—that they can-Not control--so now Here--Alcohol could well help to create unwanted 'actions' of "Elder aboriginals-- which _may be_ behind much of 'the sexual' abuse as seems to still be rife today—even though there are laws to prevent such abuse.
Here again-- I have personal experience-- our friends have for many years—been 'Fostering such young aboriginal children'—They recently have returned a young aboriginal child—after they were asked to *"take care of the child"*--So then for the past Few Years—they set their own life aside to provide a stable home and care for this child—as—

The substance abuse- parents were incapable of giving proper care- and were obviously a danger to the young child-- <u>the activists would say</u>- **the "Stolen child."**
This Childs *'substance abuse'* parents could not be trusted to care for the child — so our friends have looked after the child until- the parents had proven to be able to control their own bad habits — control their substance abuse.!
Same-- I guess with the lovely "aunty Jen" who I found on-- The Net-- she apparently- is a carer for her 6 grandchildren as their *substance abuse* parents are unable to properly care for their 6 children--<u>It is not insinuated</u>--these were also one of sexual abuse — but--recently I saw a TV Report + read it in H/Sun newspaper that —
Three <u>'Brave'</u> **young aboriginal women** — were **publicly *pleading* for help** — asking for 'Someone' to help them get away from their "family groups"-So rife with rape and sexual violence-- <u>maybe</u> I Say- likely to be a result of alcohol/drug abuse etc- ? These young women are refusing to join in such *'a family group activity'*--wanting to avoid rape, and sexual violence- then being pregnant to some "Elder" family mentor etc. To not want to become part of 'numbers' and "statistics" — or- become part of 'records' of — The aboriginal girls/women — who had become 'hidden victims' of tribal sexual violence.! Such as was reportedly--a problem back in "the 80's"- **Hence I <u>guess</u>** *"the nasty words".!*
Here these young women felt they seemed to be 'doomed'-

This is a <u>copy</u> of a photo of the three **Brave** young women who were so concerned for "their future" — they tried a very public--appeal for someone to help them--Here one can use the word **"Brave"**- with these women- for speaking out and not wanting to be caught up in this age-old scenario — Yet now fearing any reprisals. Where these young women-- have realised that "a better life" can be theirs and they don't need to sit around with their extended families--to wait for someone to Rape and- Sexually abuse them--till they become pregnant. Yes- it appears to still be a problem today. <u>All of which</u> — also makes me wonder--how many of those children-- born into that Original- side of aboriginal groups have already died--because their parents didn't join with--*'the other side'*--

Those as "aunty Jens" Group.? Who had opted for progression with The Govt. -To now-- where many are drawing some type of Super or Welfare payments whilst others have also learnt to earn a living of their own--which was another reason why this group decried the Govt. with their crap--"*stolen generation*" claims-- Yet-- it obviously still seems a problem in "normal" aboriginal life today in 2023. To me -tho- "activists"- blame lang Hancock for some *nasty words*- 40 years ago — albeit they don't print 'The Question'-- but as you will read herein I do seriously distrust what these people do re-present — and have seen more than once- where vision and words are "altered" or "dubbed" and whilst I also doubt the man was '*an angel*'--but as you will read herein many times-- we will see and hear "things" that maybe-- weren't quite- as they seem.! Even so- **none have the right-** to- Blame--any children for what any parent may or may not have done--maybe said or did not say 40 years ago--
No way- not on.!
But I have learnt "these activists" don't care about the many-- $$ Millions Gina Rinehart AO — and the Hancock prospecting group — have paid to and contributed to help "Aboriginals" — They don't care as long as it--*fits their agenda*. But also- then-- I must say--IN their defence--*though they may not deserve such--* but- as I explained — **I am one of the few alive** who has been trained and lived with--Use and the practice-- Of the "elders" type of **"*brainwashing*"** and to these people -Well- an old saying could well apply as:--"*don't judge him- as he knows not-- of what he has done* – where here these "activists" led by--

Such continual ***"brainwashing"*** as was and still is — being handed down by the "Elders" in "<u>made-up stories</u>" could well fit this bill.

To then another opposite example — as I do explain where I found the wonderful "aunty Jen" as I have not yet met — but as I mentioned — she also appears on a web site — and had years ago obviously joined "the govt. System"- and as Capt. Phillip said <u>would</u> happen — She has had a job for decades-- has 'super' had a lovely house — a car-- had children--now as 'a carer' for her 6 grand-children- <u>on the net</u>--she is pleading for the govt. To give more funding--to help her care for her 6 grands-- which their parents apparently are not capable of doing safely- which to me-- beggars <u>questions as</u>: -- First what is happening with 'welfare payments'- of the parents here.? Then — how could "aunty Jen" and her 6 grand-children- all still at school age--and their 'flawed' parents — ever have survived-- if they had remained as a part of the "other"- *No — stay as we are* group of "elders" who still use **"brainwashing"** to continually fill the minds of young aboriginals — promoting 'ideals' such as- *fight the invaders- drive them from our land--force them from our land.!* Which is- now so 'Old hat'- that it isn't even funny.! **<u>Yet they won't admit:</u>** — that if--Descendants of the "First fleet" those as they abhor and try to be totally rid of- But IF — they **had not been here in 1942--**the Japanese **surely--** would have Massacred <u>the whole aboriginal race.!</u>
Yes--I know I am <u>re-iterating</u> — But--Spears and nulla's Vs- Guns-bombs- armed planes- <u>yeah</u>- fat chance--great defence.!

THEN it's "the elders" who are continually driving their whole race to demand-*"change the date"* of "Australia day" *change the date – because waterloo creek was the worst massacre in aboriginal history – this day brings back sadness and pain and memories of The Thousands of Our Ancestors Massacred?* Where "activist" writers/ reporters "all jumped on the band wagon" – as they wrote that 300–to 1,000's were massacred **at waterloo creek".!** When-- my **Real** Research says-- That is all--Total Crap **because –**
        There was NO massacre **–** at waterloo creek at all.!
It is an "elders"- long ago created total genuine "Furphy".! Logic- I say- **simply as:--** it would not have been possible to have 'massacred' 300 to 1,000 aboriginals –
First-- who--were not there.! Because my research shows:-- they were not there -- to be massacred – or then IF They HAD been there--to be Killed--Then for NO Bodies to be found.! My research shows:-- it's a dead set – "Furphy".!
        We have all been well and truly-- Conned.!
**The aboriginal race...have been Conned--
By "their own elders"** for 185+ years.! But now – maybe-- "the magic" of the revered professor Lyndall **Ryan** will find the bodies – maybe – they will all be on her "massacres map".! Her group say "they have 'found' where many **massacres** did occur"--they are all on Ms Ryan's massacre map.?
Except – Oh--oh – NO – No Sorry –

They have found No bodies or body bones either.!

148

No- they don't say they found Bodies or any- Body bones—
Either--It is interesting to note—at Any of those 174 Sites.?

I examine- **the waterloo creek "Furphy" in next pages** –
and—I Point out that IF—as the 'elders' have always said—
the waterloo creek massacre **was the worst** *massacre* in *aboriginal history* –

then it makes their other claims Become--nothing but—

Total crap.!

Because- there was- NO massacre at waterloo creek—
It's an Elders long ago-- made-up— BIG "Furphy"-
The Irony of all of this- is unbelievable—

Because-- no one ever questions it –

No One-- ever asks—

Where are ALL the bodies.?

DID You ever Ask—My Reader.??

Keith Windschuttle's --
"the fabrication *of massacres* of
aboriginals"--

Yes--it IS weird — because they use all modern IT- Latest Computers- TV- including in the government funded ABC- Universities – etc. As they and their families live in top quality housing- either supplied by govt. Or paid for- by their higher- than normal salaries and subsidies- as most carry on- to me--such **deceitful** weird activism.! Most of these <u>are</u> "activists" and-protesters- taking part in any type of 'movement'-- as are intent on trying to destroy the people- the Govt — as they are being Paid by —

This- I see--is — just **so weird**--I mean yeah- **so weird--** which I really do have trouble getting my head around these things-- like 230+ years since captain Phillip landed in botany bay to build a colony to house overflow of British convicts- mostly guilty of crimes as steal a loaf of bread or similar- which of course- logical thinking people would understand that-- this is why the first fleet--did not include soldiers and lots of guns and why--totally contrary- to- as "activist's" would have us believe- that- as I read recently-- one said--**ever so positively:- I re-iterate:-**"*there was armed conflict- from--day one — we fought them then — we still fight them now"--* again — **as I point out-- totally--mis- informed** — and as-- for all my long life- **the aboriginals have claimed** that they were the <u>Original</u> Owners of this land — But then after experts did the DNA of <u>Mungo man</u> - **Suddenly in 2021 without a whimper--**<u>The Elders admitted-</u> That they were Not the <u>Original owners</u> --at all — but they are now "The Custodians" of this land. All which I say is also **"<u>weird</u>"** because with so many aboriginals being--

151

"Massacred"-- one would expect Someone — **Somewhere** — would have at Some-time- even "stumbled" on a group of aboriginal skeletons or body bones — and had done DNA tests--but No-- it seems Not so--Not in 200+ years.!

So- my interest grew when I researched many of The Claims to find an unbelievable web of confusion — with so much misrepresentation- so much 'repetition'- like *"claimed deaths with no bodies" over and over--*and then I read that much of this was-- and is-- being created by the highly titled and the so respected "truth teller" elder 'Professors'-- who have been working-with universities for years- again- Paid for by-- The Government.! Yes- you and I — have been paying them-- **It's a crazy cycle** because-- their titles even to honours from the Queen (rip)--then books--reports--movies- most of them have published for own profit - and all have been helping to form **the disregard** *within the minds of the young aboriginals — helping- for generations to create bias — and untruths —* always-- Against The Govt.

For those who have read their literature — listened to lectures of/by the "experts" who do talk as **if they really DO know-- as IF they were there--is** why--they Do know.?

But--of course- *we know*--they were **not there**.!

The problem as I see it- actually began 'way back'-way before movie maker Andrew Pike and aboriginal wife Dr Merrilyn Fitzpatrick- with Professor Ann McGrath decided they could tell the story — or- could tell **"Their"** Story-- better in movies- No not true "factual" events — but **"Stories"** which subtly --Created false images and false impressions.

Causing False thoughts--in the minds of the thousands of young aboriginals- who were being *Totally Brainwashed-- Totally misled* – Which then it follows that sadly – The next generations believe-that what they are seeing-hearing or reading by/from these trusted 'truth telling elders' **IS true**.! And so- they then have built their life and beliefs upon this material – which – right from the start were **Not The Truth** but--just **made up** "**stories**"- told by really Good Very **Fantastic** "**story tellers**". Much of the material- they did say- gained by interviewing "Elders' who could **not have actually been there either**.! But they were "told"- by their "Elder story tellers" who also used "*historic-imagination and narration*" to produce **their own** "***good stories***"-*to then pass these on via their "dreaming"*--**Oh boy – what--***real smart cookies those "Elders" were*** – *because they created – their "dreaming"* – *then extended to "Dream time stories"*--*where*--no matter what "the story" was--it was never ever-- going to be based on 'True or Factual events' – to always be made up facts-Made-up "stories" to tell- A Tale – as sadly I see "stories" that- since then-- millions of aboriginals have *been reading and-- believing* – because-- the tales were made to seem real-- when passed on within their "*dream time stories*" which then-- all the next generations *respectfully*--**totally believe**- what their "elders" told them--yes--they believe out of Respect. They believe if- an "elder" said it – then **it must be true** – they wouldn't tell **fibs**- or wouldn't tell Blatant Lies--would they.? Ironically as I do demonstrate herein – The Elders and- their "*dream time stories*" always were--

153

And still are — The very worst likely format of "made-up" facts known-- and surely are responsible for "the attitudes" demonstrated by aboriginal activists here today.!
Now-- I have always believed--there are two sides to Any Story--and also — that where I see- smoke--generally there is Fire — but-- then — Here- everywhere I looked- trying to write a true- feasible story-- based on "Facts"-- I did find even more confusion and more contradictions — and except for Myall Creek- one site in WA--The 7 bodies killed by Nunns group — None of these "stories" did ever involve actually *finding Of Bodies*- or *body bones* etc. Then the more I looked the more I read the more unreal contradictions I found — then--the less I could ever believe any of the so called "Experts"- or- their books- or- reports or literature- as Eg: -- the things they wrote- such as:--"*they drove hundreds of aboriginal men women and children off the top of the cliffs*"-- like- Oh- wow could a Reader just "imagine" for a moment what a horrific and tangled mess of bodies- that would have been — imagine the horrific screaming- the cries of pain- the agony and suffering **IF**--*it had really happened.?*
Yet- not one of the "expert storytellers" has ever Queried One word of that "Statement".! Nor ever asked- Hey what did happen to the Hundreds of dead bodies — were they all dead--what happened to them.? Or — why were none of those many hundreds of bodies Ever found there Why Not.? Where did those 'dead bodies'--ALL **Disappear to.?** Was it aboriginal- *black magic.?* Did aboriginals have some —

Mystic powers that made bodies magically- "Disappear".? Same as opening statement of the esteemed roger Milliss book which says--*"they marked the occasion by slaughtering up to 300 aborigines etc"*- He- as with henry Reynolds--wrote books- 200+ years later--yet to write as if "they were really there" as if they knew—as if- it was A Fact—even- like 200 years later "come-on"-Up to 300 massacred--They were writing 'Crap'-- Made-Up Stories- well I Guess-we could say-1 or 2 is- up to 300-- right.! But that is not what these writers were trying to convey- No.? To me--**they wrote--utter crap--**all--made up stories but--Really "the problem" was that- there was **No Preface**—On Their Stories—They did not *First advise* their readers that what they wrote- was--just *their own-* made up stories—their own opinions-- but then again- No Readers Ever Queried them—and not one ever reported "Finding" any of those (up to 300) Bodies- NO- they **just "disappeared"**-as if by "magic".? Well- I guess that—my research found that they supposedly "Appeared"- as- if--By Magic.? So-to later Disappear—as if--By "Magic"-- I guess is ok.! But again- problem is *the "dream time stories"* then told this to young aboriginals who all naturally "believed" what their elders had told them-- because—if "the elders" told us- then we know-- it's definitely True.! So-again none did ask--what happened to the bodies.? Yet now 200+years later--"stories" of Body Numbers-of those "massacred" as are being claimed--by prof. Ryan—yes- Just 200+ years later---even- 'Renee' said:--

155

"Kevin--*I work closely with historians- and I can tell you now- many massacres were never recorded... Why would they record it right?* **To Me-- the** *"why would they record it"* bit — just doesn't make any sense — that sounds to me--like what-- 'an Elder Historian' would say- if they don't have solid evidence to put forward-- to be considered — like a body or two.?
It's not like — a woman not wanting to record a rape — where she believes that no one would believe her- yet she must go have The Doctor to examine her immediately. BUT here IF-- it was *'a massacre'* then there would be bodies — Who could Not Report that — here it would be someone else who would Report IT — Then presumably — would have to decide what to do with The Bodies — would they Bury them — Mark "The Spot" Or what.? No- this type of comment makes no sense at all — Because when The Settler at Myall creek — saw what the raging Gang had done to the 28 native people — he then Rode A Horse-380 Klm off to Sydney — to be sure *this atrocity* was reported and followed up on — ultimately- the 7 culprits were caught — Tried and in December the same year — the 7 were hung for their heinous crime.!
So here, to me — like first I would ask — how did this historian learn of "the massacres" — like who told them-- because we are talking 185+ years ago — so this information would have been passed on from "the Elders" which means like 4 to 8 generations = 4-8+ Versions Of The Story--so what would any one of those 'Elders' or now "the historians" have to gain-- by Not to Record 'a massacre'.? Nah — to me —

This sounds very much as there was nothing to Record and could easy have been One of those listed on Ms Ryans "massacre map".!   All to me, seems much as what I am writing about herein--where 'Renee' is likely the 6-8-10th in line and yet she talks to me as if — whoever did tell her — had seen it actually happen Yesterday — OR as IF- She had Seen IT.! This exemplifies exactly what I am pointing out — that I see it is incredible how successful this "elders <u>*brainwashing*</u>" has been- as here 'Renee' could only get this information from 'A Chain' of Elders <u>*made-up*</u> stories — and yet — she is so totally IN Belief of what this 'Historian' has told her — with No evidence to support the story which is absolutely incredible 185+ years after an event- I say <u>*likely may Not--ever have happened.?*</u> Yet 'Renee' is sure of this "massacres" information — because An Elder has told her — and still the numbers keep growing--and with <u>due respects</u> I say — She is a 'Perfect example' of the Totally **brainwashed** people that I am talking about herein. **Yet she is unaware of this--**which is incredible to me — but no matter--each time the amazing thing is with each 'new massacre'-again--<u>they still find No Bodies</u> — *surprise- surprise.!* I find that this is un-believable — to See how successful this <u>*Brainwashing*</u> still is — as the younger generations are so fully in belief of what the "Elders" have told them — way beyond and above whatever anyone could ever have imagined. Today — the absolutely amazing thing here is — that if I were to say — *No I don't believe this* – then I am Bias or Racist — or as 'Renee' says-- 'I am Gaslighting' the statement — when —

To me-- 'It'-really would be just another example of so many of those "*made up*" stories as I have been talking about.! Because naturally—if there were No Bodies then- **there would Have been NO Massacre—And there would be- nothing to be 'Reported'--** Then it just adds to the tangled web I have found within my research for this story.!

But again "*the common thread*" IS-- **How did 'Renee' know.? The answer Yes of course is--**she was "Told' by her "trusted truth telling elder" (historian). *I can only assume that they did tell her-- about the mangos — before the tests of the DNA arrived or before the infamous* **"Confession"** *from the elders in 2021.?*

But all of that aside--because a massacre was not recorded- However--that should not stop anyone from later--*finding bodies or body bones*. But I guess--they didn't report finding those either.? Again--I wonder why.?

I mean—when one looks at any of these 'things'--logic just seems to be something that no one ever appears to use or understands—same as "the big deal when professor Ryan— began her "massacres map"—I often wonder—what type of "Application" must have been required to warrant the govt. to Approve "a subsidy" to produce "a map" of unknown Native "massacres" and—who would have approved such "funding"- and to Not say *"we want you to find the bodies too* .? And why would producing bodies or body bones—not have been "a part of the deal".? Same as I suspect- 'Renee' did not ask *"the historians"* —like Ok-- so it wasn't recorded-- but **what Did happen** to all of the bodies or body bones.?

Did these just *"disappear"* as if by magic also.? Or where were they buried.? It is just So amazing — that none ever query the Statements.? None ever asked for <u>real proof</u>-- these are the things I Have found- that I can- not get my head around- just can't understand why —

None of the younger generations have ever questioned--any of these incredible "off the cuff"- type impossible "claims".? No — <u>I don't understand it — at all</u>.?

Like if I were in 'Renee's' place--and someone of authority told me that — ITS *not like- hey I don't believe 'they won by 20 goals — can't wait to see the report on that game.?*

Then on Monday — we have the report in the paper — and we have the real scores.!

No- it's not like that — this is quoting something that may have happened or Not 185--200 years ago — the answer won't be in the next day's paper--

So- I surely would be asking *"where were they killed--and how many — what happened — do they know who did kill them.?*

Where are they buried or what happened to the bodies etc" — did they hang these culprit/s too.?

Yet again here- obviously "Renee" as others with her did not ask — and here again-- she has passed on **'Factual'** Information as she learnt by **"here-say"** and I would be expected to Believe that it was true.?

So **then**-- I couldn't help but- be referring to comments--as I earlier had read within excerpts from:--

<u>Keith Windschuttle's</u> --

"the fabrication of massacre of aboriginals"--

As he says:-*"there is a lack of awareness in details of frontier wars- because Australians are too embarrassed by them.!*
War is typically associated with the right-wing and for this reason-- Left-wing historians like **henry Reynolds** *who--have written about-- Secret "frontier wars" against aborigines have found a sympathetic audience with others of the left."-*
Keith Windschuttle's-- *"fabrication of aboriginal history"--* released in 2002--in which he demonstrated that **Reynold's-- had misrepresented** evidence to justify the existence of war/killings/massacres. He said *in one example* – Reynolds had cited primary sources when giving accounts of **10,000** aborigines being killed by colonists – however- when he (Windschuttle) – had checked citations, he found that Reynolds **made the figure up**--cited it--as if it were 'a recorded fact'. Basically, **Reynolds** had gone to newspapers and counted – the mentions of attacks on **white** settlers by aborigines he then multiplied his figure by 3 added 20% to decide how many aborigines had been murdered-- by whites. Reynold's did not justify why he used that ratio--nor did he clarify that his citations were referring to written records of- whites killed by aborigines--rather than the opposite.?

Newspapers of the time often criticised colonial governments for **not retaliating** after attacks by aborigines-- which could mean that aboriginal deaths are lower than colonial deaths. If the military were not retaliating, a good argument could be made that the colonial population--**simply did not have the capability--to kill large numbers of aborigines. As firstly, guns were in short supply.**

So much so, that when convicts later rebelled against the authorities in the 1804 castle hill rebellion, they did so--using 'pikes'.

My research from there- I guess- made me 'focus' on what was being <u>quoted</u> by most of the "experts"-claimed to be aboriginal writers and the many aboriginal historians — trying to learn if someone — had "claimed" to have "found" bodies and- or —
Had found body bones- to support " their stories —
<u>but alas</u>- apart from Myall creek--a WA site and the 7 that Major Nunn - had shot on way to and at waterloo creek--
<u>I could not find such</u> — to support those aboriginal deaths or claims of massacres.!
Yet--there are many proud aboriginal "activists" — who I see have genuine intent —
But they still *"fight the British invaders"* (the govt.)

Because they have totally believed all of this **made-up** 'Crap'- **as is** being fed to them by the so honoured and/so titled incredibly so revered-- "Elder experts"-- IS true.!
I say this because —

I found they are being so badly "misled" so badly "Conned" by their own — *Trusted* 'elders'.!

MISCONCEPTIONS-

My research found so much *misconception*--hence --
My 'theme' –is- **"truth" and "facts"** where I found--
'the power of *truth — telling*--reveals--
Not as aboriginal "activists" try to imply — but-- instead it did reveal--the greatest "Furphy"--ever seen- as-I reveal herein- **So** now-since I started to write about"the aboriginal story" I have constantly found so much "misrepresentation"- so much confusion--people intentionally trying to create "misconceptions" relating to 'mistreatment' of aboriginals — Till after perusing "keith windschuttles" book- which he wrote- about *"fabrication of aboriginal deaths"* etc. Since then literally everything I have seen — I first sadly do auto-distrust — before it proves to me — that it may be- or- is true- here I present various examples to show what I have found- as eg:- The Photo on next page is featured by- I think.? A very unsuspecting *louise mcnaughton* –who 'found' this on "pin-interest"- I have not met Louise, so--*am not sure if she claims to be "aboriginal" or not.?* But I suspect this photo was presented here- intending to demonstrate *"in-humane"* behavior toward aboriginals — when this person first did not study/reseach the photo very closely — before passing it on.! I since have found that it is a photo taken at the 'wyndham prison' w.a. In 1902 which was meant to show 'in-humane' treatment of aboriginals- in early 1800's--I include more 'photos' and 'sketches' within this section. Each one having been *posted on aboriginal web sites* aiming at convincing readers of "the in-humane" and/most "barbaric" manner in which "early settlers" or soldiers had mis-treated aboriginals during colonisation from 1788 into 1800's — examples obviously lodged by aboriginals to prove the british 'invaders' were massacring the people and stealing their lands- **destroying their culture**. So not to deny there must have been-- Some "things"we would not want in our Lives--

But—I read these were caused by both--whites and blacks-**although** most writers are only interested to show the aboriginal side as they do here-as eg:-- This photo is-- no doubt meant to look *deplorable* because-- well a **picture— is worth a thousand words.!**

Here--most will draw **only- one conclusion** from this treatment Depicted as being from early **1800's** right.? But then I checked--

<u>The picture</u> is said to be taken in 1902. I say likely later so – here is **another** *"made-up"* **story.!** If- to take- <u>a Second look-</u>

I see <u>questions</u> **as like** — IF it is to show 'things' as done in 1800's --who took the photo **in 1902**--and why was 'the mock-up' made and Why was it shown.? What 'conclusion' did 'they' <u>want people to come to</u>.?

Here-- *we see* — *what <u>seems to be</u>*- 7-12 aussie aboriginals-- Captured--sitting quietly with handcuffs and neck rings locked on and linked with chains, and <u>one white</u> <u>overseer</u> who seems to be un-armed. **There is no reason given** — as to why-- these people are tied/chained up- whilst a handler has what looks like a key to open handcuffs--

<u>all quite a dreadful scene</u> — for genuine people of today — who try to understand how this type of "thing"--could have happened — way back in the early 1800's — yet this pic was taken in 1902.? *"a mock-up"* **for sure** — but why.?

<u>**I did ponder many things**</u>--then--we do find so much of aboriginal history — is full of these manufactured "<u>*made-up*</u>" "facts" — and **here I query:**--

   * maybe it was taken later than 1902 — and ARE they Australian aboriginals.?
 * **the clothes** worn by the overseer don't appear to be as the settlers/marines wore in early 1800's in aussie.
   * one could 'think' "a Cruel overseer" would be armed-- 'a gun' or 'a pike' hanging from his belt.!
   * **the natives** appear 'too relaxed' and complacent — just as if they- 'posed' for the photo-- <u>as they did</u> .?
   * to look at the "photo <u>flash</u>" back then- it would have- made them 'blink' — un-accustomed to camera flash-- or — the flash would have reflected on faces.
    * the 'lock' on neckchains is like as made mid 1900s.

Then — *if we look at* **"the background":**--

The corrigated iron- garage roller doors behind them--most likely **were** not manufactured-- **before 1944--** in usa.!
I am not surprised as much or most of aboriginal history — as- the "activists" claim-- as do historical writers "Stories" tell us of-- are I have found- built on--un-truths and/or "made-up" facts- as here- often misleading such as here--
    yes--a picture — is worth a thousand words.?
Because most people Do believe what they see.!
    Or--will believe--what they--"Think"- they see.!
Then —
I wonder how much the 'aboriginals' got paid-for the shoot.? What were they paid with--and-
Why would anyone want to try to *mislead* us-- like this.?
As- I found there are many 'official' reports of aboriginals-- most by aboriginals--where again--it appears that the stories presented albeit as 'the written word'--no matter if correct-- a fact--or just the writers personal opinions--actually these are what has become **"Our history"**-as no one has ever Disputed their claims —
So we have a history built on *'made-up'* **Stories-- not facts.!**
And--then looking at the next photo- **I ask how could a** young **'aboriginal'** first gain such a 'Special' cocking gun — when everyone else had "brown Bess' Blunderbuss load and tamp 2 shot long barrel Guns- reports said as were used till **1874.?** Then--who could have taken such 'a photo' of an aboriginal obviously **intent on suggesting-** this was taken way back in early 1800's-- with this gun-- which had not even been made as early as that.? Because reports say- this gun--would likely not have been available before **late 1890s.** Then most images- way back there- were generally sketches drawn-- then Coloured in by 'pencils', as the sketches on next few pages demonstrate It is this type of *"made-up"* facts as I chose my 'theme' **the power of *truth-telling* will realise change**

Things shown in those pictures--can my readers truly <u>imagine IF</u>--major Nunn with 20 marines/convict mix- even had such a rifle as this — how they could still possibly have shot and killed 1,000 aboriginals — **No- I really can't either .!**
<u>Logic would say</u> = 1,000 natives would mean est. 450+ able bodied aboriginal men — with spears and nullas- with max- 21 shooters- on horseback — in a confined creek — <u>Nah</u>--
<u>It would be more likely</u> — the 450 would knock the riders off the horses and kill the 21 riders — and even before they had fired many shots — because-they had the front-end load and tamp- long barrel **2 shot brown Bess blunderbuss — not as the one shown in this photo.!**
Then-the 'prints' on next pages are also of some misleading Sketches-- as "the activists" had distributed-- **to prove — Prove what.?** When "activists" — feature such photos/prints sadly it means- <u>None</u> of "the Elders" of today — descendants

Of earlier "Elders" had **any Idea** of what *the actual truth was-likely had No Idea* of what 'the truth' *ever was-Or did not really know- if-* maybe anything actually Did happen-at All- way back there- The attempted **deception is absolutely incredible** as **in** the sketches on these pages show- all which are featured in aboriginal literature/web pages- with intent to prove that:--
"the waterloo creek massacre" of 1,000 natives--was real.!

This 'print' is likely-as an aboriginal artist "saw" take place-- from what the artist was told — by some 'Elders'.!
But in reality--*in this sketch* — there are likely 20 aboriginals and maybe 5 soldiers shown at a site where there are hills.? But--there were No Soldiers there at that time- as obviously this is **at the wrong site** as the waterloo creek area **was Flat It had- No hills — No big trees close.** This was drawn maybe just a-Century or more later--by someone- most likely being — Guided by *'truth telling elders'* as passed it on- in *"dream time stories"* as **'the teller'** didn't know the correct details either.? And--1838 guns were long 'muzzle load 2 shot —

Brown Bessie blunderbuss' the guns in this sketch would likely not have been issued pre-1890's--the sketch was likely drawn well into 1900's--**intent to "Prove" 1,000** aboriginals were **"massacred"** at waterloo creek --

But to my eye--**the sketch-** shows an impression- exactly **opposite** to as was intended where one rider has been felled and other 4 riders are greatly outnumbered--total confusion as the sketch is intended to depict *the opposite* story- then--

*Here--I ask--how could anyone look at **this sketch** and see-*other than an aboriginal mob with spears attacking-- a group of 4-5 troopers on horseback-- who have guns — the huge number of aboriginals would win easy — they would kill all of the riders. Maybe those are 'the thousand' as were said to have been "massacred".? **Here- yes-** I Do see **a** "massacre"--Of Whites.?

This **next sketch-** is where we see 'Settlers' not soldiers in the Cabin--as clearly shows 8-12 aboriginals attacking 3 settlers who have guns. I can see--one white is speared--2 aboriginees are shot.? The guns in such an attack--would normally "kill" the aboriginals--

But *in reality*--this sketch also--**is basically incorrect**--

As it would be- more likely that the aboriginees would kill the settlers--**because** not many of the settlers had guns—and certainly not the later model winchester as shown here--so-- whoever did the sketch- and who decided to use this **to Prove injustice or "a massacre"** of aboriginals--when yet again this-- *is actually showing the opposite*--with so many aboriginals-- the whites--are clearly defending themselves- *from* attack by the aboriginees-- but that is not-- how the reporter people are calling it--to them it comes under same heading of-- **"massacre"** of aboriginals—

Here in this sketch-- again they supposedly are showing how their aboriginals **were "massacred"** — by settlers — yet when we look at the aboriginal guerrilla-warfare style attack here--

We can only see *the exact opposite* and in such open attack-- to charge and not have checked if settlers had guns- as shown here-- the **settlers did have guns-- this could only mean--** aborigines attacking guns with their spears and boomerangs/ nulla nullas etc the whole group would have been **SHOT-- Some maybe Killed--** but "self-inflicted".?
Because settlers are in the shelter- **albeit** I found no example of settlers building such "shelters" which look-- more like "humpies"--but the settlers are clearly *"defending"* their group A Result I see--is nothing more than--**a self-inflicted** massacre with likely--no settlers hurt or killed in such an attack.
But- again most of the settlers didn't have any guns — and--
I have seen **no evidence** that settlers built any such shelters.!

171

AGAIN-- all I see here is-- just more examples of aboriginals and/or "activists"- creating more misleading and/ or false entries. Trying to convince the 96.7% of our population – that the stories as they have created are 'true and correct' – trying to boost the numbers of their ancestors who were massacred or slaughtered--by the British – as they continue to do these things--yet always from the other side- at the same time-- they are talking of "reconciliation" – which all adds up--
to – more confusion--
which now means that all talk of "reconciliation"-- is--and always has been-- **really total crap.!**
Because *definition of reconciliation is- an act of "reconciling"-- as when **former enemies** agree to an amicable Truce.*
Where--again this is so much crap because **'the enemy tag'**-- could only apply to the aboriginals--who- forever--have regarded the British as an enemy. **Because** the British from way back--don't see the aboriginals as their enemies.!
They hope to see everyone -keep working to-- **"a united-Australia"**- with every aboriginal enjoying being within-- "the system"-
But in saying that--I know that many- would not have ever even 'thought' about it like that – It's Not what "The Elders" will tell them--and they would have "trusted" their "elders" even at their own detriment – and then just follow what "the elders" have said--looking back--it has been obvious that one part of the aborigines have thought of nothing else-but to destroy the "descendants" of "the invaders" – totally ignoring the Darwin war – not ever to concede that the British **Saved their lives**--when they fought and defeated the Japanese army- in Darwin.! Instead- their total focus it appears is to be we will just use "the invader- descendants" to help us regain Our Ownership of The Land – then we Can regain--
Our Culture.!

To Own "the land"--so then--they do talk with "forked tongue" — which means--nothing has changed.!
Yet in contradiction--many thousands of aboriginals-- have fought side by side with the very people--or brothers and sisters of the descendants of that "First fleet".!
So there--my point- in writing this book is to say that-- in my opinion **you can't** "realise change"- when telling the truths-- from One side- from One point of view — or-- from infatuating the minds of your kin--with king sized *"Furphies".!*
That can only be justified if--you did not know they were selling You--a *"Furphy"*-- so from here on--the organisers of our "Museum's" will be faced with choosing One only feature- or- One highlight--or if not--then as the Indians say- *they will talk truth-- with 'forked tongue'--as their current format- won't work anymore.!*
The aboriginal web sites say:--*the dreaming means our identity as people. The cultural teaching and everything, that's part of our lives here, you know...it's the understanding of what we have around us-- **the dreaming** has different meanings for different aboriginals says **Merv Penrith**, elder, of Wallaga lake, in 1996.*
Regarding the waterloo creek massacre- we do know that-- **Five white settler men were killed** *first-- which was why-- Major Nunn- was sent to arrest and bring the killer or killers-- back to trial.!*
But another says:-between 120 and 300 aboriginal people of the Kamilaroi nation were shot by major Nunns (group)which was at waterloo creek and became the largest single massacre in Australia.? But--we just don't know-- where all of those people would have come from--or what happened to those 120-300 bodies.!
My sums say:--20 guns max. x 3 shots per minute = 180 shots- in battle x 35% accuracy at that distance =max 63 hits--fired in rapid-fire- many would miss--as in such a conflict —

Where spears and nullas were being thrown = bullets would be unlikely to kill more than 10-20.? But wait--Lieutenant Cobban- and 2 settlers went behind--found excess aboriginal weapons--means 3 less guns = Possible Shot = 7- 13 or less.? I include all of this banter to show how there is so much chaos and confusion--*the web page continues with:--*
the exact details will never be known as are no official records- only **unreliable** *accounts from* **perpetrators who** **were scared** *of prosecution after-* **murderers of- myall creek** *were punished. (hanged).*
I say- **that logic is Odd** — Typical- as its clearly not researched because. Eg:-the "waterloo creek massacre"-was supposed to have happened on **26 January 1838**-- but--
the **"myall creek** massacre" of **28-** DID happen on **10th June 1838--** which was 6 months- **after-** waterloo creek supposed "massacre"-and--
Myall creek Judgement was not given till **15 November 1838.?**
So- I ask:--
Why-- would 'they' be **"scared"** of **'a penalty'** as had not even been Ordered — Had Not happened yet.?
Statements from eyewitnesses said- lieutenant Cobban *claims he & 2 others- rode to the rear of the group and found a large cache of aboriginal weapons in the bush and secured them. when he returned to* **the river***, he had seen* **Two aborigines being shot***, trying to escape- and believed that* **at most three or four** *aborigines had been killed in the conflict.*
** **I Note:--**not a massacre-"**A Conflict"**- another Report said-- Sergeant john Lee was with main detachment of mounted 'Settlers/ Marines--that pursued the aborigines down **into the river.** He then claimed that forty to fifty aborigines were badly killed. **I Note--**
  ** a river--not a creek.? "into the river". Sergeant john lee *reported*--I ASK--how do you "badly kill" anyone--in a river —

When this "conflict" was supposedly carried out at Waterloo creek — and Nunns group shot 10-12 — but also killed 7 of the natives.? THEN — Nunns Group was made up of Mariners and Convicts — NOT Police — or Soldiers--and in her appraisal prof. Lyndall Ryan at the university of Newcastle had said that--*"sergeant john Lee's " version of what happened-- is the most reliable".*? Yet-- it- appears that 'Lee' was not sure if they were at "the waterloo creek"--or at "the river"-BIG difference there. Minor detail.? No-- just more confusion.!
Because "waterloo creek" would not have been a deep creek-- now been dry for many years — now just some 300mm deep- So again- I got confused--in the **further irony** that--I couldn't find any "records" that showed where such a large group of people- could have been killed (black or white) on **the 26th. January 1838**--anywhere.?
And--to stage *"a surprise attack"* on Nunn's camp site- that morning--it would be likely to have been by the 13 released with maybe 5--10 others--any-more surely would have been Heard- which would have also meant *No surprise* at Nunn's Camp--plus--if there were 40-50 natives- in the attack group- then I would have expected there would have been some of Nunns group killed — or wounded--but Only one was Hurt.! Which in itself--is odd--to imagine that even 17-20 could "attack" 20 of Nunns Group- By Surprise --and not kill any.?

Then-- there was--Myall creek--June 1838-
Which — whilst the type of killings are not what one wants to hear of-**to me-**this surely *was the worst slaughter* on record — Yet again there are Two Versions as:-- When asked by the station hut keeper, George Anderson, what they were going to do with the aboriginal people, john Russell said- *"they were going to take them over the back of the range and frighten them"*. The stockmen then entered the hut, tied them to a long tether rope- largely women, children- and old men- which they--

Led away-- they took them to a gully on the side of the ridge-- many metres to west of the station huts. There they set about slaughtering them all- except for one woman whom they kept with them for the next couple of days.
Then 28 people were murdered- as women, old men, and children. Ten younger men were away on a neighbouring station cutting Bark. Most of the people were slaughtered with swords as George Anderson, who refused to join the massacre, clearly heard there were just two shots. Unlike Anderson, Charles Kilmeister joined the slaughter. Testimony was later given at trial that the children had been beheaded while the men and women were forced to run as far as they could between the stockyard fence and a line of sword-wielding stockmen who then hacked at them as they passed. They then Be-Headed the others.
After the massacre, Fleming and his gang rode off looking to kill the remainder of the group, who they knew had gone to the neighbouring station. They failed to find these aboriginal people as they had returned to Myall that night and left after being warned the killers would be returning. On the party's return to Myall two days later--they dismembered and burnt the bodies before resuming search for the remaining people- after several days of heavy drinking the party dispersed--
A Different version was--When the manager of the station, William Hobbs, returned several days later and discovered the bodies, counting up to twenty-eight of them- as they were beheaded and dismembered- (Not Burnt) he had difficulty determining exact number- He decided to report the incident- but Kilmeister initially talked him out of it. Hobbs discussed it with a neighbouring station overseer Thomas Foster, who told squatter Frederick Foot — who then rode 380 klm to Sydney to Report this massacre to the new governor George Gipps- who was supported by attorney general John Plunkett who

Ordered police magistrate-Edward Denny-day at Muswellbrook- to-- investigate the massacre-The 7 Culprits were caught- then — Tried IN Court- and in December--they were eventually Hung.

Now--in most aboriginal lore--they refer to tribe- clans or just a family--normally to be of 4-6-10 to Live in each "Humpy" with likely 4-6 "Humpies" in a group with similar groups in another areas-- There were reported to be 250 various 'tribes' or clans around Australia--with the highest number being in The Gulf of Carpentaria area- due to Fertile ground growing their food — better and more frequently.

SO-- how many 'natives' were here in 1788 as eg:- To start with- there were Higher and Lower Figures stated — SO If to say the number of 470,000 total aboriginals were in Australia at the time of "the first fleet" landing--less say 40% of those in 'The Gulf'- that leaves 282,000 were amid 250 'clan's' spread around Australia--

My Sums then say- it's likely there were maybe 1528 to 2,500-- in the Sydney area--

SO--Claims of "*Thousands* massacred".? "*Thousands*" died from disease — and *Thousands* were shot by Soldiers — would appear **NOT actually Possible.?**

But- Few "Activists" it seems ever do Check their un-founded Claims — because IF they did tally all Claims and tried to then deduct all of these claims--From the total number of Natives — IN The Sydney Area--they would likely not have *"thousands"* there-- to be killed.? So--then anything that the descendant's would claim in this area--particularly during Captain Phillips time of 1788-- 1804--would likely have **NO Grounding at all**. Later moving into the 1800's under new Governor's--Land was being opened up for Farming--as they were pushing toward the now Queensland borders--breeding cattle and Some sheep for wool--Reports were saying many more of--

The aborigines where in this area--and there were many more problems--however property owner/farmers reports said — they did also employ some aboriginals and many 'Clans' often were 'Camped' on some of these properties--often giving guidance for Settlers--   As they were 'mapping' new water holes - creeks and Rivers etc in the surrounding areas. Then-- 50 years later in 1838--there was also lots of un-rest recorded-- as the "elders" of the other 200+ clans began to React to these people using "their land"-- Many settlers and their staff were murdered--due to the aborigines revolting to these lands being taken over by settlers- Such as-in early January 1838-- they had killed 5 stockmen/settlers — which was why Major Nunn with 20 troopers- made of Mariners and Convicts was sent out in Retribution--to settle things down--capture the killers and bring them back to trial-

On 25th Jan 1838--near the river--they arrested 15 aborigines-- to decide 13 as not connected to the killings--so let them go — the remaining two--tried to escape and were shot- not killed.

On morning of 26 Jan 1838- then a group of aborigines made- **"a surprise attack"** on Nunn's camp--just One trooper was reported injured by a spear--then 4-5 aborigines were shot at as they ran away. Later Nunn's group followed that group down the river then caught up with them at what is known as "waterloo creek" — where the ever famed/publicised and much exploited "Myth" of- the waterloo creek massacre-- supposedly took place.!

Reports say "Nunn's group" now re-armed/re-loaded--had Tracked this group of aboriginals' along the river and onto the creek--where my research shows--22 of Nunns group and an est. 25 of the aboriginal group staged an encounter-- much as the "hand to hand" fighting or battles as were Renowned in wars--in a situation as that--the guns would likely be of-- No real danger as shooters would not be good shots and--

Trying To re-load On-Horseback- would be next to being Fatal-- one officer said he saw 4-5 aboriginals shot—Nunns group of course would not be keen to admit how many of their own members were killed or wounded--But journals said that- Nunns Group had shot 10-12 Natives had also Killed 7 Natives. Which they took back to The Colony and His Report said they had pursued and captured the gang responsible for killing the 5 settlers- Bodies Laid to rest-- The Case was Closed.!

Now it could be possible that many could have been injured but my research says there would not likely have been any women or children in their group- AS it is <u>highly unlikely</u> that no more than 20 aboriginals were in the group which made the attack--or more 'damage' surely would have occurred to Nunns Group-- some would have also been killed- **So <u>My Research says</u>**--its *highly un-likely* that women and some children were there--at the creek. <u>To re-iterate</u>--<u>**unless**</u> it could have been 'normal'--when a group did attack Troopers who had guns—that they *take women and children with them*--which again--<u>I very much doubt</u>.!

Yet everyone knows "the massacre" of <u>hundreds</u> to <u>thousands</u> of aboriginals happened at this creek on **26th of January 1838-** *None did doubt it — when "the elders" said that it was:--*

    the worst massacre of aboriginal people-<u>in history</u>.!

<u>Well- I say</u>--whatever it was--or may have been-- we do know there were 2-3 shot—likely not killed--in the morning-then some 10-12 were shot in the creek fight with another 7 Killed- And after "The Conflict"--Nunns Group took 7 Dead bodies back to the colony with them and claimed they were those Natives who had earlier killed the 5 settlers—The 7 bodies- Nunn's Group claimed in "Retribution". <u>His Mission Over</u>. To me--if this had been ***"the worst aboriginal massacre"***-- when just 7 were killed--Yes-- I Would say—

179

IT probably was —

And it would have been the worst — **For all of 6 months —**

Till later- **1,294.klm** away- a group of convicts slaughtered 28 natives- old men- women and children-- at **Myall Creek —**

Which was duly reported — the culprits were caught — they were tried IN Court-- then finally hung for their heinous crime —

The 28 Bodies had been kept and were used as Evidence to Gain The Decision — In Court.!

'A VOICE'

So here now "A Voice".? And as one could expect--
Not just a simple "Referendum" – and as I read "the Official referendum booklet"- I found- nothing has changed – even on this booklet- issued in August 2023 – by the Government. Again- I see total confusion is in vogue--to start with--
The YES page says *"it's to recognise those as have been here for* ***65,000 years*** – that's a good start because for at least 200 years we were told the aboriginals were Original owners- who have been here for **55,000 years**- yet here it's now 65,000 Years.? No mention that in 2021 'the Elders' had said they were NOT the First Australians.! Because- 'the mungo's' – the experts said – Had died here **62,000 years** ago but their DNA was not the same as aboriginals – now here – Australian Govt. Say-- **'First Nation people of 65,000 years.** *On another website- who pay tribute to 'first nations people – Recently I read that-* aunty Carolyn Briggs *AM- and* Ms Cheetham Fraillon *quote that* **'aboriginals'** **have been here 70,000 years-**Yet – all are sure the voice will be ok because-- The Voice 'Committee' will include indigenous Australian's from every state and territory, Torres strait islands as from regions and remote communities – all of whom will 'advise the Govt' on things relating to aboriginals--
Then the booklet says – we now rightly celebrate indigenous Australian's and their contributions to our country-- it goes on to say "Governments from both sides invested $Billions in programs which haven't fixed problems--or reached down to The Communities? Yet they say--a Yes vote means "A better future for Australian's"- except they Didn't say--

HOW we All will BE Better.? They just ask Australians to vote YES- but they and the PM — who was elected to help ALL of us Australians — here are asking Australians to vote Yes — for 'A Voice'-without first providing them with any of the details to be able to make an 'Informed Decision' — so as I see this — that means most will Not vote for something they don't know how it will work or what it really means--so this means the "Referendum" as I can See- surely will Fail-- due to The PM not providing the detail voters require — even after Big Business has opted to declare Help, and $Millions for The PM — angling for better working Future — Oh-- IS there A Vote to happen also.? This could very well Backfire- for them ALL.

The Yes vote- to help **"the first nations" people** they refer to as "the aboriginals who want to have "a voice" enshrined within "the constitution" — to look after all "things" as affect the aboriginals "A Voice" to liaise with government — on all things as affect aboriginals — the original owners of this land. Here--I will be surprised if our bias PM — will really get his way with this shemozzle- albeit- "Houdini"-Found His way out of some amazing situations.? BUT here they don't mention that it was just IN 2021- That aboriginal "Elders" did **suddenly** announce **they were NOT Original owners of Australia** — so- they were to be known as 'the Custodians' of the land and *have been as such since* — as where anything to have officially been opened by aboriginals--they said we are "the Custodians" of the land- But here now we are asked to — Vote YES-- To Help **"First Nations"** People-

Here for **65,000** Years. Says this booklet produced by The Government — **Led by our Labour PM** — with "the activists" in tow- who conveniently have NOT Recognized "The aboriginal Elders" Un-provoked CONFESSION in 2021 — that they were **NOT First Nations People** — BUT in May 2022 Albanese took over The Role of Prime Minister and ALL immediately Dismissed "That Elders **Confession**" of Not being "First Nation People"- and NOW- Suddenly-- The Aboriginals Have been Here for **65,000** Years-**Yet No One told "Uncle Colin"** who did--AS a representative of *"The Custodians" of The Land-- duly* Bid "Welcome" to The Footballers Playing in Finals On The MCG and On "The Land" held by 'Indigenous peoples.? Welcome says Uncle Colin unmoved – Yet- in doing so – He IS acknowledging that obviously **HE Didn't get "The Memo".?**
SO- I wonder who we really Did vote for in August 2023.? It is ironic that — The Yes vote campaign leader Is Australia's PM-- who as I understood-- was supposed to be 'non-bias'- as he is representing **ALL Australians** — That is what I thought- was what the Prime Minister is supposed to be doing. Yet here **it was the PM** *who is leading* the charge for a YES Vote and is intent on not giving a chance of there being a NO Vote success — here I read--there is strong suggestions that the PM plans to use "trick questions" in his public vote call — where what-ever one answers- ultimately will return a Yes vote — Then--that surely could explain his lackadaisical approach over the past months-Aware A Win For HIS Yes Was assured-- which I find is absolutely--

Incredible because—We know that IN some countries—well some Leaders were Terminated for Less.? But a win for the Yes vote is strangely one as this leader has Set his whole career upon- that He would "Create a Yes win".! I did read many of the news reports- which are saying the No-was well ahead in polls etc- but today yet another 'trick' has been discovered where experts said as someone ticks a yes-- it will be counted—whereas if a person did place a x cross on the square to mean No--the x cross will not count as a No vote.? Next reports say Absentee Voter Forms have Not been sent out- which means even IF some did eventually use An Absentee Vote-- IT will not Count because it would be received too late.? ALL of which to me- just emphasises what I am writing about here- like <u>'Someone'</u> <u>trying to create their Own Result</u>—Trying to conjure up 'ways' to "improve their Yes vote totals by using stealth –or ways to falsify or negate other people's NO votes to make it appear false or invalid.?

This is **like-way back--the mongrels in charge-** did that to rig the weight scale—in order to be sure that 'Phar lap' could Not Win his second Melbourne cup. Illegal- yet always made to appear to be legal and legit--as the old saying goes—*one never knows what a person will do- to gain the result that 'they' want…once they are given the power of control*-- where they 'forget' what 'fairness' and "morals" were ever all about-- and what they should stand for.! Which ironically appears is likely--in this country's Referendum voting.!

Here to point out that I do also understand (in layman's-terms.) *That:--No alters or additions* were to be allowed/to be made **To "The constitution"** — unless "it"-- whatever "it" may be IS *of value- or- benefit-* to the Whole community.! So- In my simple logic- that would mean- to win 51% majority in a Referendum- could hardly be deemed as *of value to the whole community.? A Win for "PM" but Not for the Whole Community.! So- I wonder what will happen here.? And- will it be a Fair result?* Of which I very much doubt.! "Fair" of course, always depends on, which side of 'the fence' you are sitting on.!

I digress — as now some weeks later- I interject because The PM's YES-- Lost The Voice Vote-39/61%- Yes — LOST-- Very Badly.!
Now--whilst I am hot on the "rig it" and the **"porkies"** trail-- I don't want to stall my writing here but-- woah- woah-- Hey- wait up — We didn't decide — **Did we vote for the** aboriginal *"custodians"* of the land — or did we vote for-- *"the first nations people."*--I wonder.? Because IF The Aboriginals ARE NOT "The Original Owners" — and we had A Yes vote Win for **"First Nations Peoples"** — What happens then — AS "Technically" The Vote Result — Could be deemed Null and Void — and The PM has Spent $400Million of Public Money — for Zilch--because "their elders" have Sworn in public — that they are "The Custodians" — and ***NOT--*** The First nations people Not Original Owners of this land.? So — Oh boy — here we go again.? Total confusion again.? Now is also 'a good time' to just re-iterate that my research --

Found there are- already **70+ "Voices"** within government with various duties acting on behalf of all the 'aboriginals'-- Which it seems is where a heap of our problems do come-- from already — and is where there is a heap of confusion — with — Not enough attention being given to these 70+ people and — To what they are appointed to be doing — it could be that these people could already be trying to do what "The Voice" was Going to do.? It also says that both sides (of parliament) have invested $Billions in programs--that haven't fixed problems or reached communities.? And now the PM has already spent or Committed to est. $400+million to get vote booklets out to everyone — to Help complete The Voting-A figure my logic says would likely double by vote day's End- and Not One Cent of it-- being spent in problem areas.? Earlier I said:--

There were **3 main problems with aboriginals--**

<u>One is</u>--that they have been constantly *"brainwashed'* by 'their truth teller elders" — and none did tell them of this.

<u>Two is</u> — that they 'want to believe' all of the rubbish that the sensationalism seeking writers have put in Their Books etc. They even now want to use the false rubbish to teach children "Our history" at schools — approved by the writers of this false rubbish- like-thousands massacred at waterloo creek when just 7 (seven) bodies were found.?

<u>Three is</u> — the major problem that none will address — being that within the aboriginal race- there are 4 four sections as:--

    1)-the super educated professors- and top income academics-
    2)- the next level highly paid consultants — advisors etc —

3)- *the elderly – pensioners – elders who "tell stories" etc--*
4)- *the protestors- and able-bodied young- who won't work.*
Here although I have lots of experience to back my comment It appears few if any DO ever relate to this separation which- I see – works as the top 2 groups being so well respected-- Are as 'Indians say'- *mostly "talking with A forked tongue" as-* Most are only intent to "get what they can for themselves." As they use their 'positions' to "influence Governments and gain subsidies"- often it seems approved by "like officers" – to ironically fund rubbish quests as **Ms Ryans massacres map-** to prove numbers killed/massacred although – there seemed to be NO Condition that Bodies or Body Bones are required.? Yet whilst bodies were "non-existent"--Somehow The Govt. still managed to finance "protests"- which try to divide our country. In general – the activists and those as won't work just create havoc for their would-be employers – I guess these are areas where former Governments have wasted $Billions trying to help these people – to no avail. AGAIN – **I HAVE Experience here**-As example:- Last month- sadly we attended a funeral of our dear Old friend who passed – his grandchildren were 'down' from "the top end"- to say their farewells. They have a personal problem and can't afford air fares--so the Family Helped them – eg.- Their Grandson- took his family up there on 'A Contract Job' primarily to Train young aboriginals how to physically do these jobs- *He ended up in hospital with a 'nervous and bad physical' breakdown* – First- He couldn't get The aboriginals-- To come to work-- Those as then came- would not work –

The business set-up for the area—has Set Quotas—the Local aboriginals wouldn't work- so He-as manager/trainer- had to work Double shifts himself to try to meet their Quota's-- till finally he had a breakdown-- had to quit the job.!

THEN--<u>Though not personal</u>—but I read where "the elders" were attacking Miner- Andrew Forrest—where in general he had earlier Committed to employ Aboriginals—but his Local Mining is also A Business set on meeting Quotas.!

<u>I didn't Ask</u>-- but my Guess would be--that the mining giant could have had the same problem as our family friend had—and there too- The aboriginals wouldn't work--so they just hired people who would work—Because they must meet their quotas also.?

The aboriginal "<u>truths</u>" are all built upon *the truth tellers* "<u>made up</u>- stories"-and—here The Miner would be at Fault.? Lest-- that would be what "The Elders" would pass On. Yes—the trust and faith of their younger generations--and this now has all simply compounded--and--the "Historical" writers- movie makers- professors and other "do-gooders"- Senators in parliament—have done nothing other than Help create **more confusion**—in their attempts to make their own money and or gain their own Status or great Titles etc.? Which is why—the aboriginal "history" is overburdened with So much "Triple **C**"—like- "<u>made-up</u>" **Crap**—with massive **Contradiction**- and more **Confusion**—ALL of these On Top of "the Furphies".! Where I just **feel so sorry--** For the young aboriginals—who for their whole lives--Have totally believed their 'Trusted' elders—Who have literally--

189

Fed them rubbish-- for most of those lives.! The Trusted elders--who have- so badly **misled** them- and--have- so badly **mis-informed** them- and I doubt- if- having **"another voice" IN Government**-- would change any of these things for any of us- at all — and-- if it did happen — It will likely take 3-5 years-- before they even know about that.
My concern--is--will they, **Then**-- believe me.?
Leading to the situation where now I see: — **None of the younger generations**- really Do know- **what is** truth, and — what is not.? YET-- the aboriginals want **'a voice'.?**
I would say Ok — but I see-- it is not required — because I See already "many voices" are advising Government-- 'Many voices' (*who don't always tell the truth*)- So- why do we need another voice.? Another **"*truth teller*"** feeding bias information--to the government- To- have "A Voice"-- **I ask- to what end.? Would it only 'divide' us even further than 'activists' Divide us now.?**
And-was "a voice" intended that once approved- **the 3.3% of aboriginals** will They try to control the other **96.7% of** — Australians -and lead us like sheep more than they do here today.?
When there are already **some 70 'voices'** around or within Government to be sure that aboriginals are treated same as other citizens. **But then** — To want to be treated Same as-- "the rest of Australia"- to be "Equal"--I know they believe that means '*they will get more*'-- But that- in reality- **could mean**-- To Lose some of what they have now — because--

Govt. Currently spend aver. **$2.32 per Indigenous person for each $1.00** spent on non-indigenous-- So I say--on this subject, it would be wise to **consider what you Have-** which could end up being "Less"-- To Re-iterate "A Voice" — when there are- already 70+ Voices there — As example:--
   * the PM's advisory council-
   * the council of peaks- represent 70 aboriginal groups
   * 11 federal politicians — are aboriginal--
   * We have an indigenous Australians minister —

Then all aboriginals have-normal long-term support as-
   * Parenting payment-   * Job-seeker payment--
   * Age pension-   * Carer allowance-
   * AB Study- crisis/Special help —
   * Family-- Domestic violence. All of which means —

I re-iterate-- Govt. Welfare cost-- for aboriginals--is recorded as being aver. **$2.32--per--$1.00** spent on non-indigenous —

If- there was "a voice"-- What would they do.?

Who would be selected.?   Would we:--
   * reject--If they knew of — **mungo man.?**
   * yes- If agree to Honour **the Darwin war.?**
   * yes- If would praise **the aboriginals who Fought in Darwin — with--** their countrymen--
     To save Australia from *the Japanese.?*
   * yes- If will want to teach the children **our Combined history.?**
   * If will **not** want to teach all the young Australian Children just aboriginals "made-up" **massacre crap.!**

So then--who could we trust-- now we know *'the truth'*--

About the mungo's-- and we know It was no massacre at waterloo creek-- SO--**Who to trust.?** Surely- we would Not Appoint those pollies – who are trying to push the Yes vote right through – When trying to not show the real value- and all of the Ramifications as they are proposing – relating to land- and current Property owners rights etc.? One said:--Oh--all those details will be explained after the vote –

I said--He tells 'other jokes' at parties too.! He won't Tell though –
There are already est.400,000 Aboriginal Property CLAIMS waiting to be Finalised in NSW alone – One News Reporter Says.? Another said-- if or when the public get to see and then to understand- full implications as are 'hidden' or not shown yet - within "A Voice" Yes Vote- which will be discussed-- after Voting-- Is Done.?

IS WHY I would have been surprised if a 'Yes' would be voted in BUT--*Today – Now some weeks later –*
IT doesn't matter because- Min. 61% of All Australians--

61%- Have Voted NO – to The Voice.!

The People IN Power- Did STOP Phar Lap- Australia's Idol.? BUT Not Here – So I say – Surely, those 70 Voices already in place Now should be Trained/Helped- to do everything required as they were shown what to do-- what they were appointed to do – let them use "the $ millions" as are being wasted-- trying to get the public to vote yes – which will only further divide our country – that is what I see.?

Going back to 2021--my question for esteemed professors- I would ask:-- **Did you-- know about** "the mungo's".? Did you too- knowingly **"hoodwink"** us all.?

192

<u>I believe</u> likely yes-- **tha**t they had known that they had been <u>Conning us</u>-- **for all of those years.**? <u>When 'the truths'</u>--as they had always been telling- were just *"their own versions"*-- Of what <u>they said</u>- could have happened-- IN earlier Colonialisation of Australia--mostly it was what they <u>wanted it to appear</u> as <u>did</u>--<u>happen</u> — and- it **is this Crap** that they wish to pass on to **our children**- yet all the while knowing- there is **this**- <u>king sized</u> porky- **and--<u>king sized</u> mistruths- and <u>massive</u> deception**- as we now know of-- for example- To start with--there was <u>no massacre</u> <u>at waterloo creek</u>— which was never any type of massacre as just 7 were Killed-- by major Nunns group--- in retribution for earlier killing of 5 settlers.! So yes — that is hard to digest for many — but it became just so trivial when in 2021 — "the Elders" openly had voluntarily admitted- that they were **not The** *Original* **Owners**— that-one would have expected- had opened the proverbial **"can of worms"** — **shattered the lives** of many thousands of their younger aboriginals — who have always totally believed their "elders"- <u>as for many</u>- I could believe- it literally would have destroyed most everything they have believed in-- for all of their life.!

But no — ironically confirming-- they have believed their 'truth teller elders without question — Here now--it is like as though — they never even heard that **"Confession"** by their Elders — and-- They have just carried on as — IF nothing had happened — And the younger aboriginals have just taken it-- In their Stride--carried on — and well "They"-- the booklet producers and the prime minister — obviously-- they all —

193

Just didn't "get the memo"--AS was sent when the elders had **"Confessed"**--they were **NOT Original Owners-** saying that we must now call them *"the custodians" of this land-* They say we are NOT- The First Nations People — and we are just "The Custodians" of this Land — Even though — Their "Confession said/or confirmed that *"The mungo's"* story IS True which said they had died here 62,000 years ago — and we have just been here for a mere 55,000 years- it's incredible because none of this group *"Got the memo"* and here now we had a PM led Campaign trying to convince us all to vote YES- to implant a voice in parliament on behalf **First nations people** — which in itself — is all really incredible.!

"Facts"- **Nuh** — they will now--be "made up" <u>again</u> to then become the main parts **of "Our History" as will be taught to all of our 96.7% school children** — approved by The 3.3% Aboriginals--prepared with Help Of/or by the sensationism seeking writers Book Stories- with help of the un-bias ABC — as also being **Paid for by** our 'un-bias' Government.

Yet — 'His'--The PM's Referendum — ironically IN Defeat-- is now even more confusing-- because "they"--have totally disregarded *"The Custodians"* and they set the campaign — addressed for **"First Nations peoples".?** Those booklet producers with the PM and the Government- overlooked all of this — and have totally focused on helping *"the First Nations people"*- **who have been here 65,000 Years- to** Win- the voice referendum.!

YES — They Lost 'That' Battle — But yet-- It IS--with "The BIG War" still to continue--

194

To-which--again I discover is just so much more confusion-
When aboriginals- were always said to be here **55,000 years**--
Till "experts" found *"mungo man"* and said he died here--
62,000 years ago—**wow on surface-** that was **embarrassing**--
yet 'the activists' — and now "the PM" — in his Booklet are all
Still saying- First nation people who have been here for
65,000 years.! So suddenly **55,000** years *IS No more the go*
I ask—does anyone really know how long the Aboriginals
have been here.? *I point out: —*
Currently here are **the main features:--** aside from "a voice"-
The aboriginals are intent to have all non-indigenous people
"to tell the truth" about numbers massacred in colonisation —
and that 'the British — admit to- have stolen their land.!
Which infers 96.7% of the population- mainly 'the invaders'-
the First fleet descendants-- Do tell un-truths.! But IF 'they'--
Had Won the Yes vote- "they" would have it all—and then
we get to have our own *"made-up"* History taught to ALL
our school children-- Featuring 'Real' Stories by Milliss and
Reynolds with aunts and uncles—combined with "Truth-
teller elders" tall—'*Made-Up' Stories--.?*
Most aboriginals have become "activists" — they constantly
refer to "Elders"- as being their *"truth tellers"* — and as I see--
The NAIDOC theme speaks as if the Elders are something
"Super Special".? **As example--It says:**--that they are:--
*"cultural knowledge holders, leaders, trailblazers, nurturers,
advocates, teachers, survivors, hard workers as loved ones —*
Which IS Doubtless TRUE — Yet- IT pretty much describes--
My parents as My ancestors — as also most other people's--

Parents and Their ancestors too — But here- **I say ironically-** That's exactly where the "problem" began and ends.? Because--the aboriginal problem of today — was-- created by the "Elders" of long ago — as they became *"truth tellers"* who did not *always tell the truth*- and instead — They passed on- their *"made-up"* stories- and have Continued to pass these on- to many generations of their own people.!

And here now- in future 'they' will also be guiding "their"- **"made- up" History** into all Our school education modules.

In other words — "the activists" have been advocating we-- (the 96.7% of the population) must **"fess up" tell the truth--** They "attack" saying they want the non-indigenous — to-- *"tell the truth"* –IN short--They want us to believe all the "elders" porkies -- and accept their *"made-up stories"* — which is to say the least. Really- absolutely Incredible but now--

IT again will not matter because-- They are going to achieve this by- "Educating"- our children-- and to first have them believe their "made-up" stories — that then The Children will Tell--the rest of us- All of The TRUE Stories presented by the "Truth-Teller Elders" and some from Milliss-Reynold and etc so — whether WE Like IT or Not--

<u>The brainwashing continues.!</u>

Which IS Un-bloody real.!.

"The Waterloo Creek Massacre"--
The Worst <u>Massacre</u> in Aboriginal History--
An "Elders"--BIG *"FURPHY".!*

The waterloo creek massacre"--

The aboriginal "elders" say — was the worst "massacre" in aboriginal history.!
Here I say--yes- "the elders" were **100% correct** — and with the journals reporting just 7 killed at waterloo creek-- that was true — for-- **6 months** — Till- the *"myall creek"* slaughter of 28 happened--
But — what they didn't realise is that- *by swearing* that the waterloo creek massacre-- *was the worst* — when--
The Journals and my research shows a max. of 7 could have been shot and killed at- or near the waterloo creek--
That then makes *every other claim-* made by "elders" passed on to the aboriginals — surely to be — **utter — made-up-- Crap.?** Which also makes prof. Ryan's "massacres map" claim- to then also be — absolute-- Rubbish.!
Where my logic says:--
 Simply--can't have the cake and eat it too.!
Yes--my un-bias research — found a total of max. 7 would have been shot--and killed at/or near waterloo creek — as these bodies were taken back to the colony- by major Nunn.
This section — IS focused on **the waterloo creek massacre.**
I try not to be *dis-respectful*-- but a reader must remember most reports and material as has ever been presented on the subject of the **waterloo creek "massacre"--**has been done-- by "elder aboriginals" which is why people such as--
Keith Windschuttle –finally wrote--
'the fabrication of massacre of aboriginals' which was written back in 2000--long before I began to write this book--and sadly to date--I have not met this person yet.!
So 'Dizzie' & co--maybe you don't want to talk "change the date" now. Certainly--I say don't change to **the 10th. June**-- Because that's the date the **28** *were slaughtered* at **Myall creek--**

Yes on **10th. June 1838-** where the mutilated bodies- <u>were kept As evidence</u>. And the 7 culprits were chased--caught--tried in court-- and duly hung in December 1838.
So yes--**myall creek** <u>was a slaughter</u> which is all <u>documented</u> and the culprits were caught-- then hung for their crime.!
Surely--<u>No one could be proud of that event</u>--and if we are to be saying **"Sorry"--**then it should be- for the atrocities of **<u>myall creek</u>** — which really did happen.!
Same as- I say--we should acknowledge **the Real Invasion** which didn't come till 1942--and was at **Darwin--by Japan.** Because--there was no invasion of Australia in 1788.!
Yes--"tell the truth" is to be the key the aboriginal "activists" on their (likely Govt. Funded.?) Web sites say--and as I-- re-iterate--they are adamant that:--
for them-- **its** 'the power of <u>truth-telling</u> to realise change'-- "truth telling"- <u>IS the key</u> to reconciliation and recompense.?
I say "true"- but they want *"the invaders"* to tell *'the truth'* which--in hindsight — now we know about **"the mungo's"** is surely "a set-back" — albeit- it is possible that 'they' did not know — and they too were Conned by their "elders"-- yet — they still ramble on about we should *"tell the truth"*--of how badly The British- 'the invaders'- treated their ancestors and how they stole their land- how they **"massacred"** the ancestors-by the thousands –is then why they believe that they should 'regain' the land- because they are "the **original** owners" of this land- IF we don't mention **"the mungo's"**- or- **the elders 2021 confession.** Yes- <u>they know all of this — because</u> -*"the dream time stories"*--<u>told them</u> this was true.!
But-- **<u>it was all false</u>**-- "made-up" stories--A Furphy--yet they don't count **Myall creek-- <u>which was atrocious</u>** — incredibly <u>**inhumane**</u>-- **So bad**—that when 'a settler' knew what had happened - he rode 380klm to Sydney to report it-- The culprits were later caught-- tried and 7 then were hung--

199

SO to Me- this was clearly-*"the worst massacre of aboriginals"* on record — *and fully documented — is why we didn't hear about this because "the elders" then activist writers cant "make-up" their False "Stories" — and they can only write about Facts — cant blow numbers way up — because it is all on record — and it's all fact.*!

But yet *everybody knows*--**waterloo creek--was--*the worst — massacre- in aboriginals history — because the "truth teller elders"* told them so.!

Then--*The historic writers jumped on the band wagon* — *and wrote that 300 to 1,000 aboriginals were slaughtered -- yet-- I ask--how could 300 to 1,000 bodies* — *be slaughtered then--**just disappear** — That IS--of course--if-- they had been there* in the first place*.? Because-my research says* — *Those-- bodies just weren't there* in the first place*.?*

But--*"the dream time stories" are a Very powerful medium.!*
As example:--
the story of aboriginal **"elder" polly Cutmore-** featured here in a copy of an **ABC** Interview — where Isabella Higgins*- ABC- - national indigenous affairs correspondent and **specialist** reporting team's* Sarah Collards *post--at 25 Jan 2020 at 6:00am* updated *on-- 25 Jan 2020-12:17pm--Says:--*
"Ms Cutmore- was told by her elders *that"*- her ancestors were ***massacred*-- in--the waterloo creek--**"*they were shot and killed, didn't know what was happening, in this very spot- they were killing babies, and women--***Ms Cutmore said-*** *this report is an example of 'Elders' total* **Brainwashing-** *as-sadly what "The Elders" had* told polly *--was not the truth at all-- this* is an example *of how powerful-the- on-going effects of "the elders"* **brainwashing** *really are-- because- polly has already been telling her kin about this massacre* — *as since 185 years* — *the historic writers- wrote their take* — *added more numbers* — *then here now* —

Polly Cutmore-a <u>Gamilaroi</u> "elder"-says:--
"waterloo creek's harrowing past must <u>not</u> be forgotten- it is still so raw for us because there is still secret sorry business here among lots of families" she said--I feel the ancestors when I'm here"-- visiting the site always makes her very emotional -and-she chokes back tears as she recounts-"stories" <u>she was told</u> by "<u>her Elders</u>"--about ***"the massacre* of her ancestors"** here at **waterloo creek** — and I say again — that HERE also:--
The <u>un-bias</u> "reporters" un-wittingly pass it on for thousands of others to read- yet-didn't ask- *did they say where All of the bodies* were buried--where she could find her family-bodies.!
Or to ask Polly — Logically--<u>IF thousands of your ancestors</u> - men-women-and children were all slaughtered 185 yrs. ago - Logically then-- **How did You--Come to be here Polly.?**

HERE — There Never IS an answer — Because This IS- a result of constant 185+ years of continual **"Brainwashing"**-- which never did feature logic — never "did the sums"--as I know that Polly nor the ABC reporters will NOT believe me when I say **my research says:**--Fear- not Polly- your family were not massacred here at all — And there were **No bodies here to bury-** No –
But again I say "Polly" also-- did not ever ask--things like- *where did the women & children come from*--or- *where were their 'Humpies' built.?*
Did the killers burn the humpies.? Or did these people just *Appear* as if- **by Magic**- then when they were killed—
Did they then just "disappear" as if **by "Magic".?**
Did you ask the elders-- *what happened to the 300 to 1,000 bodies.?* **But**—No—my research found--No one ever asked these type of questions.
So- I say — don't worry any more Polly because it is- highly un-likely any of your family-- died here--in this creek.!
Isabella Higgins report continues:-
Today, waterloo creek- the site of the killings bears no obvious evidence of the murders or massacre. It's simply a dry creek bed that cuts through drought-ridden farmland close to the town of Moree. But again here —

Neither 'Polly' nor "the astute ABC reporter team" did logic- how 20 troopers on horseback--and long barrel- single shot blunderbuss guns--could herd 300 to 1,000 aboriginal men women with babies and children--all **into a group —**
Take their weapons--then say-
Now please "stand still" --while we-- Shoot you all.?
NO — They Did Not use 'Logic' — Nor did reporter 'Higgins' (An Aboriginal) say IT was —

"The Site of The *supposed* Killings"- No- She wrote it as IF-- She too--thought **IT WAS A Fact**--SO Then Thousands of Others Read That Report—THEN--They Too—Now Know that- IF It is written—then-- IT IS TRUE and so—**The Elders Brainwashing**—Continues On—Because these Reporters Did Not seek to find some LOGIC—NO—They reported- just looking for more ABC Sensationalism.!

Yes **Here**-as historic writers- Reporters such as 'Ms Higgens' by writing- as they DO—Then create 'Impressions' as would have Readers believe- Pollys Ancestors *did all stand still*- and So—they- all of them--had been shot and "massacred"- **Just** as "the elders" had said. YES-- that is **AFTER- they read it all- in the books**- or saw it In the Videos Or at The Movies Of Course- AFTER They read The ABC *Non-Bias* Reports.! But neither 'Polly' nor "the astute **"Aboriginal" ABC Team of Reporters**"-- **did logic** that if "the bodies" of 300 to 1,000 of their aboriginal Ancestors--HAD -been massacred- and then-- Had been buried **in This Shallow Creek**—

Surely Rains would have washed all the sandy ground away and the bodies or body bones- then would have been found- Right.? That is- **IF- they HAD been there** in the first place.? Logically--in such a shallow creek as this--someone would have found them — then checked for **DNA.**! But then — "**IF**"- **they** were all 'Shot and Killed'--*I wonder*--who could have buried 300 to 1,000 Bodies-with no shovels or backhoe-- And Who could have Buried them So DEEP — In The Ground that They would never Be Found.?

But--"Polly" knows *"the massacre" was-So bad- that to even think of it--brings back pain and suffering--brings back bad memories of those as were massacred here by the settlers from "the First fleet"*- **Because her "Elders"-- told her this.!** Yet--'**Polly's**' "elders" didn't tell her what happened to the 300-to 1,000 bodies.? When it was *the worst massacre of aboriginals in their history--* **I wonder why.?**

But NO--I am sorry "Polly"--they have **"brainwashed"** you-- There was NO Massacre — this-- **is a great** Big Furphy.?

To clarify:--

I do understand--why "Polly" genuinely does believe that this "Porkie story" is true because she has been *brainwashed* Totally Conned by her "*truth telling* elders" —

AS it appears they often told her of 'the massacre' — but they *Never Did Once*-- tell her where the bodies were buried.?.!

And--although we have not met — I am not being facetious as I say- I genuinely--Do **feel sorry for "Polly"**--because as I said earlier- I come from a Big family — and my dear cousin recently passed and unlike 'Polly'- I was able to stand beside his grave--drop some Rose petals down on his coffin- confirm "my feelings" for him- and say goodbye- To also know- that his remains will be there- next time--when we go back to my home-town--I can visit his grave, and whilst- there — I Can visit all of my family and their families too —

If I want.! <u>My real concern here is</u>—that Polly will--or has already been passing all of this Crap On--to her family-they too will also believe it is true—and continue to "pass it on"—Because--Their "Elder Polly" told them—**and They had all read** The ABC Reporters Report- **so They know It was all True.!** The "Elders" said- waterloo creek massacre was-- *the worst massacre in aboriginal history--*

When it IS all- just an "elders"- great BIG *"Furphy".!* NO- there was NO massacre as 'Elders' claim on **26 Jan. 1838—at Waterloo Creek—or anywhere else.** My <u>records show:</u>--the 5 stockmen were killed earlier- and 7 aboriginals were killed in Nunns exercise to seek Retribution But--no other bodies--Of aboriginal or whites were ever found or--reported as being found--**at waterloo creek.?** Because-- there were <u>most likely</u> **not "300"**-and <u>definitely-</u> **not- 1,000** aboriginal Men women and children--actually near- **the waterloo creek site.!**

As <u>my research</u> says the aborigines were the same group who attacked "Nunn's camp" earlier that morning—and it's **very unlikely** that any women and children/babies--would have been there--nor- would have been in the earlier group-- who had attacked "Nunn's camp" that morning— **Unless--**

IT could <u>be Normal</u> for women, children and babies- to be-- included in- **"a hunting group"**- going to attack known <u>Armed</u> '<u>troopers</u>'—which I would- **very much doubt.!?** However—If one could try to imagine how cumbersome those long-barrelled guns would have been in a close—or crowed area--then--**trying to re-load those guns**—pour powder in barrel- drop shot in—then- pull a rod from under the barrel and tamp it- put a cap in- Tamp to be ready to shoot--**Doing all of this-- whilst--on horseback as The Natives were throwing Nullas and Spears-- At Them.?**

My thoughts would be that the Rider either would fall/or be tipped off his horse--likely to be <u>an easy target</u> for a nulla or boomerang--a sitting duck for Spear--then all to be killed.
But--just try to imagine—say 20+ aboriginals on foot and 20 troopers on horseback—in a flat Shallow creek even without Nullas and Boomerangs—Spears being thrown AT Them.?
A bayonet attachment had not yet been issued to fit those guns.? <u>In my experience</u>- it would be more likely 'Troopers' were killed or injured—than aboriginals slaughtered.!
But today--I know young aboriginals *"faith in* their elders" and *unwavering belief* --in what the elders tell them-- is just so **tragic**- and--**incredulous when it is all**--SO False—as I have pointed out herein:--
I know—*how seriously powerful* the EB **brainwashing** *sales-- training was--* and therefore-- **I am convinced**--there is **no need for 'Polly' to** be upset--because there was No massacre -- at waterloo creek -no—**No**--her family- did not die here- They were not shot or killed here. No one was "slaughtered" here at this creek—**IT has all been part of a** "Big Con"— Directed by a **chain** of *"truth telling* elders" with**in**—**so many of** Their *"made up"* Stories"-- yes some of her ancestors could have died peacefully--maybe in the area somewhere-- I feel sure much as many others had -But--<u>to re-iterate</u>--as I said earlier--
It has all been part of a *"Big Con*—A FURPHY created way back by "the elders" as there was No massacre **at waterloo creek.!** And-- *from my research here* --
I <u>now confirm</u>--that my long- held belief-- of 'EB' as being **No.1. Brainwasher/motivator**--I am now--So Very Sorry-to admit--**That "EB"--now** I have come to learn-- **runs a poor Second**.! Because—I now see- **the whole aboriginal race**— Of at least 150- 200+ years-*have been totally and completely- brainwashed-into "believing"* that--so many of **the "elders"**--

Made up stories and porkie-pies <u>were true</u>—and un-wittingly They did pass these on to their generations to follow—sadly, as **here 'Polly' is now doing the same to her generation**—NOW—being Helped by sympathetic ABC Reporters—IN Their quest for "Sensationalism. NOT To seek Facts or to find The Truth--I suggest.! But the *"trusted elders" and now 'Polly'* using-"made-up facts"-are passing on so many of the "un-truths"-- which was bad enough-- <u>But then</u>--like adding Fuel to the flames the aboriginal Writers/'activists'/ABC Reporters/others as 'Milliss'- Reynolds and more-- kept "the flame" burning with Their versions **and** <u>their own</u> *"made up" facts* and *unadulterated crap-* bordering on-- to almost-- knowingly printing blatant untruths- as they did know these were completely **"<u>made up</u> Stories"** that they **were here** printing—Stories to suit their own purpose- where--
I re-iterate-With NO 'Preface' on Material Published--Then **'elder polly's'** un-questioning belief and unwavering trust in "the stories" <u>she has been told</u> by Her "<u>*truth*</u> <u>*telling*</u>" elders"- **is absolutely** an unshakeable- and-- unbelievably- sad- end result.? To Create and to-have such sad and bad memories and so—they need us to change **Australia day**—Because this massacre of our ancestors is So bad--it brings back sorrow & sad memories-- so much hurt with so many of our ancestors thousands being massacred on this day—<u>Change the date</u>— and of course-we-need recompense for all The Thousands of our ancestors as were lost/massacred at waterloo creek — and in Colonisation.? So many Thousands were massacred and this sadness is why aboriginals want recompense-- Today.
My research found—really it is- so bad--that if—it wasn't-- SO serious—<u>IT could be laughable</u>.?

The summary was:--
　　　* the natives killed 5 unarmed settlers—

* major Nunn's group shot 10-12 and killed 7 natives in what was labelled as "reprisal"-then the "elders" Blew It all out of proportion — then being helped by The "famous writers" and 'professors' as Ms Ryan who all added their bits till the number massacred At waterloo creek Numbers- had grown into "Thousands" — which is absolutely amazing that today's aboriginals--do really totally believe it is all true and- they are gradually convincing other Australian's- and Others around The World--to believe it too
Even though--as I earlier did the break-up of where sections of aboriginals were likely-way back there — we concluded that there were likely not "Thousands"- That could have been anywhere near **waterloo creek** — To have been killed.! Meaning *there was NO massacre* at waterloo creek — it is all just an "elders"- great **Big** "Furphy"- was all it ever was. To re-iterate--records show that- only 7 dead bodies were found — others were shot during the confrontation- but major Nunn's group just shot and killed 7 natives and these bodies were recorded as being the culprits who killed the 5 unarmed settlers--which means —
a waterloo creek "massacre" is another elders **Big** "Furphy" The journals- say this is the truth-- my research also found — To look back- it is uncanny as: —
The Elders don't talk or write about any of **'the wars'** where their kin have fought- such as WW1-- Gallipoli--right to– Vietnam etc--because in those wars The Govt--have all of the records- and bodies are 'accounted for'--
Same as in the Japanese invasion of Darwin — **a war** right on our front doorstep-- where those who fought have all been recorded — those as were wounded and killed are-- Recorded — Bodies were laid to rest etc. So *"the elders"* —

The "activists" and the Historical Writers- can't <u>make-up</u> - Their *"truth teller" stories* — they can't fabricate-deaths-- Because here- they are all-<u>ON record</u>.!
But-when we look at *"the invasion"* of Australia as they claim-in 1788 — then the *"frontier wars"*- with *'genocide'* during the colonisation of Australia — **my research found-** *these 'things'*- were not heard of- so were <u>not on-record</u> — They didn't exist- till- they appeared in "the Historical writers book stories" — being created when writers-needed to "find" something new and different-- to use as "a hook" needed to create "a feature" or "a gimmick" t*o get people to buy their books and videos--<u>Which they surely did</u>* — it appears.!

It is here within the hundreds of books-videos and movies etc-- <u>even more of</u> same- Published-- **Conveniently-** just before "the Voice vote".? Where the many thousands of aboriginal ancestors--as were claimed as being "massacred" — when they were killed within a video or within a book story — or-- A Movie- where they don't need to "find dead bodies" —

JUST as in all <u>The Old Western Movies</u> in days of TV and videos- Even IN Movies of Today- where "the hero's" shoot and kill "baddies" everywhere — then we just turn the TV Off — and all of those dead bodies- <u>are gone</u> — They all just ***disappeared*** — are then forgotten.!   We turn TV back on tomorrow- they shoot and kill more- NO One ever thinks of- *"what happened to those dead guys bodies* — we saw them shot — *They killed those dead bad guys — What happened to The bodies.?* They simply — just 'disappeared'.?.!
We used to laugh and say- Hey- *we should empty the dead bodies from our TV soon--because we all knew that there were--* **NO dead bodies** *in our TV sets.!*
Today we watch as <u>'Arnie' kills dozens of baddies-</u> then again next episode- he kills another 20- 30--as somehow--

They too--all just--*disappear*.! Yet it's strange—because--
The many "young aboriginals" also watch as 'Arnie' shoots
40-50 Bad guys—and They too- see the bodies *"disappear"*—
Where 'they" know—the bodies were never really Killed.
But Here--when their "elders" told them that "Thousands of
their ancestors" were *massacred* by--the British--way back
some 200+years ago—and the Bodies were Not Found—they
have *"Disappeared"*--The young aboriginals- believe "the
Elders" as they say YES-*"Thousands were Massacred"* and they
too Now want "Compensation" for those as were killed here.
Although they didn't have TV--but "the elders" say they
want "recompense" for the many *"thousands of bodies" which
did-- All just seemingly 'disappear'*-- just like as in "the Our
Movies"—and again- it's strange that- the young aboriginals
just Don't believe- it's Real- when Arnie shoots 40-50 baddies
But against All Logic--They DO believe IT--when "Elders"
say "the British" "massacred" thousands of Our Ancestors--
Yet here—They didn't have dead bodies either.? But yet-
they know that these "massacres were so bad that "the
activists" want the 96.7% of our population to change the
date of Our **Australia day--** Yes to change the date--because
it brings back sadness and hurt—but then--just like did
happen in the Old Westerns and all of 'Arnie's' movies
These bodies have just *"disappeared"* also—and ironically—
all of those "really bad massacres"—somehow-- just didn't
leave any bodies- either?
Logically and simply-because- they were only *discovered*
when Historical writers--brought them to life- 150+ years
later IN-- their many Books—on TV or video stories –
But then *"the elders"-added to the confusion- when they made up
their own stories — building on--the stories from the Books--and
passed their "made-up" stories on — in such a way as to make the
young generation aboriginals--Believe they were true--*

Eventually they *"found"* **the worst massacre** in their aboriginal history — Where numbers-- grew and grew-- till it is So bad-- So painful we need to change the date **of Australia day—** **What utter CRAP.!**   But of course--IF it was 'Arnie' or-- "A Western" we would just turn the TV Off — and the bodies **Disappear**— To start again. Yet- of the 1,000's of Aboriginals *"massacred"* here--the only bodies as ever found at any of the 'massacre sites' were 28 at Myall Creek-- The 7 as major Nunn's group shot and 14 at Coniston — Which are-- all on the record.

To major Nunn's group the 7 as were Killed at Waterloo Creek- were in Retribution for killing 5 settlers — Nunn took The Bodies back--Their case--*was closed*--mission complete.! Then-- In all of the stories as I have read — which are written by such sales/ profit seeking writers — and activists- I found just that one writer--*Professor McGrath- who had Prefaced her book* with--*These are just "made-up stories"* which I have written-- *using my historical-- imagination and narration to present a good read*-- *A good story.?*

Which was "a good read too"- But alas-- another as claimed by "the elders" to be as true stories- even with her Disclaimer. Yes- "the elders" presented it all as being true- and the younger generations believed this was a "true" story-- also.! So- these outspoken experts- all tell us what they do know Happened-- which is mostly just made-up **Crap** —

Just another of the *made-up* stories "the elders" have passed down-- it's **the "Elders" Crap** that the "great" historical writers have heard--then written their books upon-- or made videos and presented these in lectures and all manner of "information sources" to follow.

To report positively- It WAS-**"the massacre"** at waterloo creek-- with so many being Slaughtered — that WAS the problem —

211

SO- to ease "the pain" is Why they want us to Change the Date from 26th January--But I say—IF to Change It—**Don't pick** the 10th of July-- Because-*that day in July 1838 – WAS – When th*e worst atrocity did really happen--even though the Elders don't talk about this—but on this date--a disgruntled group "beheaded" 28 natives- mostly elderly men and women with children—But it was so brutally bad—that to Learn of this- a settler did ride 380+klm to Sydney—to make sure this was reported—the group were hunted, found and tried --the mangled bodies were held as evidence—Yes- the culprits were Tried and in December 1838 the 7 Culprits were duly hung for this heinous crime.!

It is all documented—all On record—which again—is why "the elders" don't talk about this.! And the sensationalism seeker writers do not write about it--because here--they can only quote facts.

But there- I say- IF our PM of the day, had wanted to say **"Sorry"**- IT should have been for the atrocity—The slaughter of Myall creek—Surely **the worst on record.!** *But*—it is all On Record—is why "the elders"—"activists" as historical writers- Can't exaggerate the numbers--from those 28 As ARE ALL on record--But to re-iterate--I do concede:-- That--"the waterloo creek "massacre" (of 7 Killed) yes it WAS - the worst- *for 5-6 months* --till Myall creek slaughter then happened, as myall creek became "the worst massacre" and it is *'all documented'* and so—it's all On Record'— Which is why- they don't write about this—because 'they' can-not make up their "stories"--they can't turn myall creek into other than what it was- because it is all On Record.! **Same as** the Darwin war—because this war is also totally documented—it- is all On Record—so 'they' don't write about it either. But when the profit seeking writers wrote their "*made up* stories about **waterloo creek—**

The young aboriginals sadly believed what they wrote- and they could all write- whatever they chose--because no one would have taken them to task — about any of what they wrote —
Because the young aboriginals-**wanted to believe** these 'things' did happen--wanted to believe the rubbish their *"truth telling elders"* — *were telling them.?*
Oh boy- now we have solved that problem-what to write about now — from here on.?
But of course--we have just hit 'the tip of the iceberg'-- because simply- whatever people--black or white- of today — Do-- Think that they know about the aboriginal history--it couldn't be further from the truth- if they tried — what they think- did-- or — did not happen is just not what they believe it to be- and also it couldn't be more confusing if they tried to create such.! The most prevalent part of ALL their stories is that aboriginals do think they know or-- believe that they know — Because-- their '*truth-telling* elders'-have told them-
To re-iterate:-
    A)- that *"they were the original owners"* —
        when-in 2021-they said-- they were not.?
    B)- that- thousands of their *"ancestors were massacred"* at-
        'waterloo creek-- when there was NO massacre*.?*
    C.)- that- soldiers massacred 60 natives at Coniston-
        when- were No soldiers there but 14 were killed.?
    D)- that- soldiers on horseback- ran hundreds of men
        women/ children- off top of cliffs at waterloo bay —
When there were no soldiers — and-- NO bodies were found.?
But then--
'The elders' credibility was shattered- *in 2021- with their greatest revelation for 200 years- which* just slid by *— quietly as — the current "*truth telling elders*"* **Confessed**—*that 'the mungo's' were here first--we are just "Custodians" of the land'*

They said – but of course-*that was after the experts had proven- the mungo's died here* **62,000 years** *ago- when we all knew aboriginals have been here for just* **55,000 years.**
The confusing part with 'the mungo's 'story--is 'the elders' did already know that-- but had decided not to tell us— They had decided not to tell us 96.7% of Australians-- "the truth".? As they decided not to tell their own kin-- "the truth".? Yet- after all this-"activists"-still campaign to have the 96.7% of Australians-*"tell the truth"* – about our-- their history--because they were Told--*there was armed conflict- from day one--we fought them then-we still fight them now"*- they say.?
Here- to point out--this Totally contradicts captain Phillip's Journals, to re-iterate- as he wrote:--*on landing they-- laid down their arms exchanged trinkets--danced & sang with the natives and- Later some elders had dinner with he and officers-on board ship.?* Later captain Phillip wrote- *they had no problems with the natives who camped outside the areas as the convicts were working. When food supply ships were delayed--* he had become friendly with Pemulwuy- and did contract with him — To supply meat to The Colony he also wrote that 4 natives had died- as many of his convicts had died of illness- some were killed by the natives- Still yet "activists" say and write their rubbish which totally ignores/or contradicts these journals as they continue to present their own *"made-up"* Crap.
So-the main problem with--the aboriginal history--is seen as:--the elders passed *made-up* stories down as "factual reports"- then- the next generations passed "their version" of all this- which then-*"bit- by bit* – *these were "re-created"-* by *the many sensationalism seeking historical writers* who *"made-up"*-- their own "false versions of the stories' as they wrote Their Rubbish such as-*'to 300 were slaughtered — one said to 1,000 were slaughtered at--* **waterloo creek-***another wrote —*

That 20,000 were slaughtered etc – One wrote *of the "Frontier wars"* – *as others wrote of the "Genocide" within the colonisation at botany bay--* <u>It was non-stop</u> – *with the waterloo creek massacre the centre show piece"- which was being used to 'trigger'* –
The change the date of 'Australia day' campaign--
Yet – my <u>un-bias research</u> found – that none of these things did really "happen. B<u>efore</u>- 'unscrupulous' sensationalism seeking writers – wrote this rubbish-- in their "<u>made-up book stories</u>" then "the activists" mixed their "<u>made-up stories</u>" to follow 'the trend'-- all of these- creating situations where "the truth"-IF- there ever was any- therein-got totally lost – till now no one knows what is- truth or what-- is not.! None--ever used simple "logic" here as:--If 300 to 1,000 were massacred in- a narrow-shallow creek – and No bodies- are found – <u>*That's Impossible*</u>.!   Then- IF 20,000 aboriginals – were slaughtered – and there WAS complete genocide of These Aboriginals--in colonisation- and <u>NONE of these bodies were ever found</u> -again I Say That too **IS Impossible.!** In each case – the problem always was – that when people did read **this** Crap- None asked- <u>*what happened to all those bodies.?*</u> Absolute silence –would then have been the reply. Because-there were NO bodies to be found there, either.! No bodies were found--even within the pages of Any of The "sensationalist" books or-- in their Blak videos- Oh yes- They sold thousands of copies--but <u>no bodies</u> were found--
I wonder *why.?*
I re-iterate--there is- an answer- of course--***simply that--*** *None of the obviously ridiculous statements- or the rubbish- these people wrote* <u>*was ever challenged*</u>-- *and it all sold thousands of books and videos- as it all--was intended to do--* <u>*for the writers*</u>.
But--no one has ever challenged *their rubbish* – none ever asked-- W<u>here are the bodies</u>.?
It is iconic – to say this was just like the TV Westerns--

215

Right here in Australia also- except on TV — we just saw what we thought was Arnie, John and the gunslingers kill all their attackers then just walk away-never look back- because they knew — there were really No Bodies to clean up — then in next movie — well of course-they shoot dozens more — Yet we never get to see anyone clean-up *the bodies* right — well because — we don't expect The Bodies will be there.? So then--in real life-- surely one would think — that logic would say-- you just can't have 20,000 Natives slaughtered — and to not find- ANY of those bodies.!
We **Can't have** *'genocide'* of thousands — and none to find ANY of the bodies- it's not feasible--**and to me not believable**-- Except — In the eyes and minds of "the young aboriginals" who right from early days—**WANTED these stories to be true.!**
Then when "activists" somehow were able to have this type of Rubbish put in print--this just suited "their agenda's"-- because they then-- could add their bit--and could pass it on. **PASS It ON**--To younger generations in the "*made-up stories* as IF all were being true- well-- If its written, and none ever ask or challenge it-- well it is true--right.!?
So "the elders" passed it on as being fact — and no one did ask those questions- and it then did — become--"a fact".?
And now-- It all becomes 'the fact's' that are to be included in Our history- *which is being prepared to be included in our school curriculum's*-- to teach **OUR Children** in schools. And one 'first nations web site asked me-- If I wanted to read articles such as will be presented to the children--including stories by the revered roger Milliss etc--as well as "the *truth telling* elders" — YES--I immediately--logged out.!
I could not believe that "these" are the people who are going to create the material which is going to be used--to educate our future children in our schools — the highly respected "elders and historical (make it up.) Writers —

All of whom have **misled** their own race for generations- and have **misled** all of us Australians—like forever--Yet now these people do get to teach The children-- Our history.?
SO- These people now WIN—**The Un-Winnable War**.?
Within my story about "the aboriginals"—we explore the reasons why we have such utter chaos with one protest after another with ever-present actions of "aboriginal activists"- leading the 3.3% of our population—currently 'polarising' the air waves- guiding the lives—and Future of the 96.7%- of the population- with their attempts to "have a voice" inserted within 'the Australian constitution' when most are not aware that we already Do have some 70+ aboriginal 'voices'-- within our government—Now.!
Yes- we have 70+ "aboriginals" who currently control and/ or influence literally <u>everything</u> we do or say already—and-- IT appears it is they-- who are so often disrupting things today—seemingly intent on "dividing" our population rather than as they say- *'we want to reconcile'.!*
Reconcile I see—
To obviously mean—Reconcile-- <u>on their terms</u>.?
When they show little or no regard for 'the lives'- choice or preference of the 96.7% others of a very tolerant Australian Population-- <u>This is, as I see it</u>—largely due to we are— 'a Very tolerant' other 96.7% of the population--being such-- 'a multi-cultural' based country—where, we are so very-- complacent by nature, happy to accept our lot, accept others and not complain--always seeming to want 'to assist' people who we think'- need help'- rather than trying to hinder their progress—most certainly when we see people who are-- un-aware of their own needy situation or insecurity- or even where they are likely to be hurt-- by others.
<u>It is this type of complacency</u>-- I see was part of the initial reaction of 'the first fleet" commander 'Capt. Phillip'—

On landing here- where he had found an appalling standard of-- housing-- coupled with the insecurity of daily food supply and lack of medicinal supply and services- and — with no visible security at all — it was all of these things and more- as- were the reasons why Capt. Phillip worked with the natives in his 4 year tenure — as he chose to help them- Yet ironically today-- their descendants now show no respect for his efforts of trying to help the natives (their ancestors).! Instead- they are activists who don't read and show any appreciation for his journals, and instead today "the 3.3% of aboriginals" pay more attention and belief to made-up 'stories' even as many were obviously written after 2010-- when the internet came. Yet- the captain Phillip journals- were written as 'Records' of each daily events- way back in 1788-92 —
And- I would think should be a more accurate summary of what happened-- under captain Phillips' control, I note:-- He reported that *just 4 aboriginals had died in his 4-year tenure.* I say likely--that would not include the death (in childbirth) of his friend- Pemulwuy's wife and un-born child nor those As killed later by his friend Pemulwuy — and his gang-- Today- these 3.3% are living within government structure as Capt. Phillip tried to explain would be started- for them — Yet here the activists- are constantly trying to cajole the other part of our population into belief that many thousands of their ancestors had been badly slaughtered or massacred by- "the British" Invasion --back in 1788 --and all are doing this un-troubled--due to our Australian population-
Don't really Question — why they want to do this--
Don't ask-- *why are they using their learned skills and their higher educations — created for them "by and paid for by" a government — that they all work so hard to destroy.? To this writer it seems like a great case of "double standards" as one could find.!*

Some ask--why can't they be satisfied with what has been created for them.? Why don't they recall losses at Darwin. But — none ever did ask for proof of any claims-of those massacred--as we don't want to punish any destructive "Protestors"- maybe as we should.? Because by tolerating-- not refuting their claims/or statements-- this works against US, even helps the "activists" create more <u>made-up</u> claims which will also be accepted — though the claims- are also- most likely to be <u>un-true</u> — and just more '<u>made-up</u>' stories.! So yes- we wonder why they can- not be satisfied with what has been created- for them.?

I pause to relate to some replies- I received as I responded to "a LinkedIn post"--a call "<u>to change the date</u>" as I replied-- "mate- there was no massacre at waterloo creek on 26th Jan 1838 — or any other date"--so why do we need to change the date.? (of Australia day.) But — my reply- fell on deaf ears-- Because the two people as I have been 'relating' with-- are the Exact Copy of the younger generation Aboriginals of today — who totally ignored what I said — Because they totally believe anything that their "Elders" have told them.! Here I refer to "Renee's" email reply-to me- which said:--

Kevin-- *it saddens me that we still have a very <u>uneducated</u> society in this country that for-- some reason try and gaslight the true history of this country. I am a proud first nations woman who also identifies as English. My mother is a proud English woman from Liverpool & I was raised with truth-telling from both parents.*
Not once was the true history of this county taught it was hidden.
I work closely with historians- and I can tell you now- many massacres were never recorded....why would they record it right??
Absolutely sickening to learn that we had genocide on our own soil & still people want to deny it ever happened.
Our first nations elders/ancestors are respectfully our biggest truth tellers that have carried down real life experiences & culture for

thousands of years. You wanna use the word "porkies" not sure if you are aware & read our constitution??
Australia as unoccupied lands? Wonder who put that down as facts and is responsible for that one? & only commonwealth country-- Without treaty?? This year's- Naidoc- theme speaks for our elders. They are cultural knowledge holders, trailblazers, nurturers, leaders advocates, teachers, survivors, hard workers & loved ones. No one's wanting division, **we want reconciliation.!**
'Naidoc'- stands for:--
national aborigines and islanders day observance committee
I present this reply —
because I hate one sided commentary — yet here though--
I see it is so clear that these young advocates do/and have--
believed literally everything *"their truth teller elders"*--
Have told them- and- they are "un-shaken" even after the
Big 2021 *Confession* that they are now to be called just
"Custodians"- Because The Elders agreed "the mungo's"
were here before them. Or- I could have asked "what
happened to the 1,000's of bodies".? Either way--They
would have no answers — So-then would just ignore me.?
But somehow, they can and do seem to not ever become
perturbed about those "small details".?
It is ironic that these younger generation aboriginals have--
remained steadfast after hearing "the elders confess" — that
now they are not original owners--which is incredible and
can only mean- either:--
 a)- That the elders- did not tell these young people-
   and so had lied to their own kin for ever- or-
 b)- If they did tell them — then the young aboriginals
   helped mislead Our population for 200+ yrs.
But — in the main — everyone seems to have just disregarded
the *"truth-teller"* elders 'Confession' re 'the mungo's' which
be-lies what we all have been told by the *"truth-teller elders"*

For all of our lives- as they--the younger generations parents have been ***brainwashed***--with this-crap-for 150+ years-being here passed down- each time with more vitriol- each one creating more ill-feeling against the 96.7% Australian--Population- yet it seems nothing has changed — However- from 'obligation'--I did google "Naidoc"--but- after several attempts including to ask Wikipedia — who couldn't 'Find' it I did not get to read it--then.!

Later-- I did go back-and got into the web site--but when the early info pages-- clicked on-to <u>an Offer</u> — inviting me to share some of *"the **Real** stories"* written by- Henry Reynolds and Roger Milliss with some of **the revered** *"truth telling elders"*--I clicked straight off — having read more than enough of the *"made-up stories and utter "crap"* as has been presented--By those ***'revered'*** writers already.!

But I wondered if I had read on-- there may have been details telling me where many of those dead bodies--<u>had been found</u>.? More to the point- I may have learnt- why such young and Genuine aboriginals as these proud Australians--would wish To "share stories" with these *historical writers—* Who have taken 20-30 books--That's like est. 10,500 double sided pages x 33 lines each page- in <u>each book</u> — to tell their "*made-up*" stories-- of massacres, genocide, and frontier wars as have affected-- aboriginals during colonisation- I kept asking myself- why so many words-- why so many books.? Certainly not hoping to help aboriginals- when <u>writing of the 'things'</u> as most likely — <u>Only did happen</u> — <u>IN Their Books</u>.? Writing when they had nothing but "the elders '*made-up*' stories"-and had No real evidence to go on- and write their books on.! Where one of them alone wrote <u>estimated</u> 20,000 aboriginals were slaughtered in colonisation which took another 10-20 books-to tell the writers story- but yet- did not identify <u>One place</u> where--

Some of the bodies or body bones could be — or-- *were* found. ?
Yes--20,000 killed — stories of details-- that need 20-30 books to tell--and NO bodies were found and- No burial sites were ever found-- in any of their material — and-- It was writer 'Keith Windschuttle' who wrote to tell us-- how Reynolds had made-up his numbers in one of these stories which were actually numbers of Whites that were killed and there--he stated these As Factual numbers of how many aboriginals had been-- slaughtered.?
The most amazing thing is:--that none of the stories--actually try to demonstrate where any of the 20,000 bodies were ever found-- or even where some of them were buried
I guess The Books-- could be "good stories" — Maybe good reads- written on the subject- IF first including- a disclaimer
But to write as they did about the aboriginals story — it then becomes nothing more than-- **utter** Rubbish —
Particularly when none of their- stories did ever explain the-- Minor details like:--who did- or how did- they destroy or Burn--the 2,500 aboriginal homes --the humpies.?
That those-- 20,000 aboriginals had lived in. Eg:-It's reported up to 8--10 natives lived in the bark and clay humpies--yet even at waterloo creek-- if there were 1,000 aboriginals--it was recorded that there were just 20 in Nunn's group — Who was supposed to have massacred 1,000 natives — They were not trained soldiers- Yet this infers each shooter would have had to kill 50 natives each — with their 2 shot long barrel tamp and load-- Betsy blunderbuss rifles.?
To follow 'the calculations' then — that means to somehow have their 'Targets' ***"stand still"*** long enough for each of the shooters to **"Re-load"** 40 to 50 times — also remembering -- these guns were rated at 50% accurate-- for 'trained soldiers'--So this equation — is one that none of those writers had even given-- "a thought to"--when they were writing their- Crap--

About this--**the worst 'massacre' in aboriginal history**—
Just '<u>minor</u> details' YES…same as if were 1,000 natives—
Occupying the area for a few weeks/or months—
Then there would have been 100 to 250 humpies built in that area…but—none of these writers nor The Elders have ever covered that- *'<u>minor</u>'* detail-- did not write to say who and how they did erase all such humpies as this:—
None wrote to say like who had destroyed all the humpies or--how did they destroy the humpies- did they burn them.?
But--none of these great *"<u>truth teller elders</u>"* nor ANY of the 'Historical' expert writers- bothered to mention any of this-- NO—These are just **M**<u>**inor details**</u>—
TO Ask *"how they destroyed/or burnt the humpies to totally eradicate any sign of the 1,000 natives"* — None thought of that.?
Or the **2,500 humpies** *where those 20,000 had lived.?* Nuh— They Have- No interest — that's just- <u>minor</u> <u>details</u>.?
But—that is what I would have expected would have surely happened—IF the <u>massacre</u> story were true.?
Because MY logic says that after they had killed all of the natives- they surely would have destroyed their 'humpies'- Destroyed them-- to eradicate all signs of the troublesome natives—
Of course—that is- **IF- The Natives- had really been there. ?**
Just <u>minor</u> details…hey.?
Now- with such writers and "elders" presenting all of their "True—Rubbish"—
To our children in schools—**The One thing that we could Hope for-- IS--**
That Our Children will be *"Smart Enough"* to SEE Through all of this "Made Up" CRAP—
Because Reality Here now is that:—

      No one—will <u>really ever know</u>--
        <u>what is</u> truth, and—<u>what is not</u>.?

"OUR History"

"**Our History**"- one would expect- comes from 'our families" — and our ancestors--which Britannica defines as:--
ancestor/s: -- *a person/s who was in someone's family in past times : one of the people from whom a person is descended*--

Eg:- My *ancestors* came to Australia -at Lorne Victoria in 1878. There is a record of what they did — who they married and of how their/my family — grew from there. All ironically reared and later buried in 'Victorian cemeteries' since then.

To look at producing **Our Australian History-** to include aboriginals- is-- well--more than just difficult — because all we have are "truth teller elders"- and their "made-up stories".? Then as I asked "elder polly"-with so many thousands of your ancestors being slaughtered or massacred — How did you get here.? **W**here did you come from.?
Like which of those Thousands of your Ancestors did manage to survive to then create-- Your Descendant line.?
The Fact is — logically each aboriginals direct descendent line — would not have HAD "Thousands in it" to be slaughtered.!
So — where did her great- great-great grandparents come from.?
How did her great-great grandparents Survive the massacres.?

Today-the problem is:-- the current generation of aboriginals- Don't have that "Line" to refer to — and everything they believe they know — about ancestors and of their history--they have been Told about it by their *"truth telling elders"- in their made-up stories* — And by reading the made-up stories written by the sensationalist writers as Milliss--Reynolds etc with SBS videos and movies- and recently the likes of Blak- video's and then-- the lovely 30 year old *Thelma Plum*-with her *"better in Blak"* songs ALL reflecting *"memories of the past"-'memories' as were told to them by "truth telling elders" because* there are No Real Facts.
So- They ALL are relaying the "Elders" made-up stories — Relating to memories as have been told to them- by their--

"Truth telling elders".? But there is no evidence as can back up their stories- yes- that in itself is the difference with the 3.3% as distinct to most of the other 96.7% of our population-- to many families-- I mean—we all learn from our parents—*but – well most as myself – we didn't have a 'trusted aunt or uncle'- telling us "made-up" False stories- we didn't have constant messages trying to lead and guide us – lead us to believe other than-- how our families lived etc- Yes – of course we all inherited nanna's & mums "Special" cake and other recipes – none ever did highlight- if there were any illegal or bad things to have happened IN Our Family--there were normally some records to find – to later be able to confirm or dispute such--*
But somehow it seems that the aboriginal elders were different-- because they were intent on passing on ill-feeling and vitriol in any form—to discredit "the invaders"—which is quite strange when those as captain Phillip had worked with in Botany bay area—obviously were doing well till 'the death of Pemulwuy's wife an un-born child—which as I see—was the Trigger that set the 'elders' from the gulf area—to campaign against 'the British invaders'—and from there—the elders have not always been telling their people *the absolute truth – as I can See IT.*
Like the aboriginals were told of- **the 'massacres'—as waterloo creek--by the "elders"**—when only records relating to those killed at/or near waterloo creek were 7 natives as were shot- in retribution- by major Nunn's group—for the natives first having killed 5 un-armed settlers—there were no other reports- but there were "Many Stories" by writers—who included Sensationalism to sell books-videos. As one said- "to 300 were slaughtered"- then "the elders" added their "made-up stories" and numbers shot up to more than 1,000 as were "massacred" **at waterloo creek**--ironically most writers—story tellers—didn't really have any idea of what sort of "Creek" they were writing about- as indicated by the sketches I included earlier But—their writing was not questioned- no Sketches were queried-

None of them.? No one asked- <u>IS this true</u>-- and so this then was accepted as being true and has become A Cornerstone- of the aboriginals history--so potent that later then "activists" do petition to even *change the date* of what is now Australia day— Because—they believe what their "truth teller elders" have said—they are positive that this did happen—yet the only bodies ever found—or reported being 'found' were those (7) seven as Nunns group had shot and took back to "the colony" to show as Retribution for the 5 settlers as were killed earlier. All the result of "the elders" and their "made-up" stories--and where none asked for "proof"--none asked—where are the bodies.?
They had <u>the writers of novels-books-movies etc</u> all of which were written/produced because it is *<u>a popular subject</u>* and as such-- the writer could be **assured of many sales-** good profits- provided they did create "a good story" — **albeit a *<u>"made-up"</u>* story—not facts-- just** a **story** to be a good read.!
The writers some 150 years later-- never thinking of whom they could be embracing when they have made statements such as *"the soldiers- shot them all dead.!* It could have been their young friends 'father—uncle or grand-father' they were writing about- As they were just called 'natives'.? But- most wrote of 'soldiers' as being those as had shot them--when in the main there were no soldiers—then they went from bad to worse because they then began to suggest 1,000 aboriginals were massacred—when they had no solid evidence except--"a story" from the elders—who 'told' of how these things *<u>they knew of</u>*- had happened—because *"their elders"* had told them--IS why they know that is what had happened—bodies.? Oh No- none ever mentioned anything about "the bodies".? It was "the thing" —they were all killed—slaughtered or massacred—but none mentioned anything about the bodies—or what did happen to The Bodies.?
<u>Minor details</u>—surprisingly enough—none were ever asked—*"what happened to all of those Dead bodies."*?

So then- this was and still is-- what the writers have built their stories around-- its' even the same today- with the SBS- the Blak-Movies- the press and the unbiased ABC — now joined by singer 'Thelma Plum'- who all keep growing The Stories but none ever ask-- about the bodies- as each time they then just keep on--expanding- on the Numbers killed or as have been slaughtered in their own *"made-up* stories" with a view to growing numbers of those slaughtered or massacred- further and further--Lord knows where it will all end, as if just 20% of *their claims* were ever true--then we ran out of 'natives'--
IN The First 75-100 Years.!

But--somehow — **they just don't get it** — Like *even my blasé comment to 'p' on LinkedIn-- went through to 'the keeper'- as I said — "mate--when I speak to you- 'p'- you are not there- mate — cause when I did a tally of all of the aboriginals as were claimed to have been massacred- slaughtered- killed etc then when I checked it against those stated as being alive in 1800's-**there were no aboriginals left**— so-- Technically--you are not here mate.?*
He didn't comprehend-- what I was talking about.?

Somehow — none of these 'activist' aboriginals here today — who keep on *"making up"* stories of those as were massacred those were slaughtered etc — like Ms Ryans massacre map etc- *None have ever seemed to add these numbers up — where they would then maybe realise — hey this just isn't right--the aboriginal numbers **ceased to exist** 100 years ago--somethings wrong here*.?

No — somehow- they just don't seem to think like that-- but — myself having been an exponent of **"brainwashing"** — I do understand how all this works. And in these people--I have found the perfect examples--who have been Totally 'brainwashed' for likely all of their lives they are completely indoctrinated into belief of whatever *'the truth teller elders'* have said- IS true — and so with these people- I knew that it wouldn't matter what I say — it will fall on deaf ears —

But it is simply that these people "the **3.3%**" simply do and say "anything" that-- Will help them to be able to run this (their) country — and — they can't/or won't ever see it-- any other way.? They make No allowance for what "The British" have actually Created on the land- what they have built- <u>for them to share</u>.? Which many are doing so-- nor do they consider what would they be doing now IF--"The British" and we "others" were not here.? The answer likely could be- **THEY--wouldn't be here.!**

No- <u>they hadn't even thought about that</u>-- they just say--*"they want their land back — but they mean — they want to "control the land"* — **as it is now--***fully developed as now-- including all the cash flow with — all of the 96.7% of population living here- creating the cash--flows of spending and taxes etc —* Albeit--they all know that this is not going to happen.! And that when they say *they want their land back* — *so we can return to* **Our Culture** — they surely must understand 90+% of the aboriginal population — just could not survive-- living like that--because they were born and bred with all the comforts of modern life-- Yes they could do this- could 'rough it'--for a weeks- holiday — but to live like that forever- NO Way--**It's a** myth — they couldn't do it.! And to survive with NO Fortnightly--government welfare payments-- Nah.? So then--<u>what all this really means Is</u>:--

That- somehow- I must write this story — I must help these people understand — because younger totally <u>unsuspecting</u> aboriginals- **have NO Idea-** that they are all being "totally ***brainwashed"--***and badly *misled* and being badly *conned* — By their trusted "*truth telling* elders" — who don't always tell the truth--Yet they are so strong in their belief of any of the things-- that the "elders" have told them- and now tell them today — So very convinced are they- that- IF their "elders" told them about anything--**it must be true.!**

To me — this is <u>so heartbreaking</u> to witness this travesty of--
Truth and the misleading nature that these "so trusted"--
Elders have been mis-using — and are still filling the minds-
shaping the lives of their younger generations- who literally
do trust and believe-- <u>every word</u> the "Elders" feed them.
Now — this has created a massive problem — because the first
nations people are organising--"making up" For the schools
To Learn--Our Australian history — to be taught to children
in their schools — except it's NOT of our history-it is putting
together "the history" of the aboriginals-to feature 'stories'
of slaughter and massacres in colonisation of the country-as
written by milliss -reynolds- marr etc-- using *"made-up
stories"* from their books — which have written the "First
Nations History" within their made-up facts — like milliss
said 300 were slaughtered-- the others said 20,000 were
slaughtered — then it was Genocide and Frontier wars-- and
all things as likely only happened IN Their Books — so then--
These are to become *"the true "history"* of Australia as This
Group- are planning to teach our children at our schools.?
Their so trusted "elders" did not tell *the truth* about the-
"mango's" discovery **before 2021** — or--
Have not tried to explain nor enlighten them about it since —
so they surely must know — to re-iterate:--
their '*truth-telling* elders'--have told them:--
    a)- that--*"they **were the original** owners"* —
    <u>when- they were not</u>.?
    b)- that- thousands of the *"ancestors were **massacred**"* —
    at-*'****waterloo creek***-- when <u>there was **no massacre**</u>.?
    c)- that- **Soldiers massacred 60 natives at Coniston**-
    when <u>there were **no soldiers** there</u>.?
    d)- that- **soldiers** *on horseback- ran hundreds of men
    women/ children- off top of cliffs at waterloo bay* —
<u>when there were **no Soldiers**</u>- and n<u>o **bodies were ever found**</u>.?

Then--'the elders' credibility was seemingly shattered- here *in 2021— with the* **greatest revelation** *for 200 years-*
Which just slid by-- quietly —
*As-*current *"truth telling elders"* **CONFESSED**- *when they said--*
'the mungo's' were here first — -we are just "the custodians" of the land'-- **but—**
Yet--these and more are what they will be including in the history of our Australia—for school curriculums--
And—
Once again—no one will question these things—because it has all been seen in writing—
In the history writers books and as such—
It will be accepted as a true account of the things as have happened—
Darwin.? Where is that—
Oh- it's another part of the country.! They will not question why Darwin should be included.!
And **that-to me- is- so amazingly bad—and really sad.!**
And—it definitely-- should not be so.!

But- **aboriginal instigated—no one will Challenge it—** then—"Uncle Colin"—'on behalf *the custodians* of this land'-for **55,000 years** will go on with His *"welcoming sportspeople to country"* — as our esteemed Prime Minister and aides are totally committed to push 'the yes vote' —(even after 61% of The Country Voted NO.)-- to have **a first nations "voice"** in HIS Parliament to represent **the first nations people**—who have been here NOW (He says)--
For **65,000 years.!**
So Now—
    who could possibly be confused—by all of that.?

CHANGE — The Date —

WHY.?

As- I say- there are--millions of <u>live</u> reasons why our "Australia day" celebrations--

Should be--**shared**--and--we should also--**Celebrate** this day <u>together</u> — because:--
 I have <u>listened</u>--and- I have been searching--
 I do <u>understand</u>--'the truth' of 'the mungo's".!
And--for all of the *"change the day"* people--
who cry- change it--<u>*because*</u>--it coincides with-
"the worst massacre in aboriginal history" —
My "un-bias"-research- says-- <u>*you were* **Conned**</u>--
There was NO **massacre** at waterloo creek.!
 Or-- anywhere else on 26th January 1838--
The *"dream time story"* tellers need **to** 'wake up'-
 Need to *'change'*--their "<u>stories</u>" asap.
Need to talk **about honouring** *all of the brave people who fought and saved us* in the Darwin war *in 1942.!*

233

I say--we should compromise- because-when--we compare "losses"--I find--we-- should be equal.!
But--Australian 'prehistory' is <u>confusing</u>-and yes-
I do--believe those "activists" who featured the words:--
'the power of <u>truth-telling</u> to realise change'-
<u>On their web site</u>--are--featuring these words — for a very different reason- and for a different cause- <u>different result.</u>?
And--here I point out--as already witnessed —
that to-- complete my story here--I have *'<u>re-presented</u>'* a large number of reports --and many comments relating to this subject--not to be- in- or used in the mould of "plagiarism"-- but to be <u>the means</u> of finding "the real truth" relating to my subject--and to--at the same time be able to demonstrate how "Historian writers and "reporters" so often do differ to my own opinion. They do *"exaggerate"* or *"miss-quote"* or as I-- have found on aboriginal web sites where they have <u>dissected</u> early Governors reports and — only refer to the parts as they believe helps them-- 'tell their story'- yet as I said in each one- I still found they had included the words as-"Retribution" which then be-lies what they are trying to convey.?   Again — yes- I say-- so confusing.!
These so often-done so poorly — yet here I believe done so- knowingly- intentionally and trying to add to **"The Myth".** Wherein I have tried to include- who did write such reports or comments--both in seeking 'the truth'--and--making my own comments--as also--often--to demonstrate just how confusing--and--misleading- and often — how *irresponsible*-- many of those reporters have been--ironically since way back in 1800s.! I say this is to all "indigenous people" because the real event- is-or--maybe something- you don't really have-- **"a clue"** about you only know — what you were told by Truth Telling Elders.!

234

Now--before I started to write this story — I found it hard-- to believe that "the activists" were so determinedly — "single minded"--that they had no more than "the elders" <u>dream-time stories</u> to draw their information from — proving how strong the "<u>dream-time stories</u>" +"brainwashing"- is- and has been because:--really--how could anyone seriously believe that after 230+ years of-"*fight- get rid of the British*" (now the Australian govt.) That — this attitude by people- saying or believing that "they" do represent the **3.3%** of aboriginal first nation people-- who live on this land — and that **this rubbish** really still does continue.? Like it appears to me that these people have never seriously considered — things like--***What would we do with it***--if we did regain-- "the land" — **Seriously--***what would you do with it.?* Because — every one of these "activists" are working and living in modern day circumstances-- have cashflows — own homes- businesses- mortgages- family-cars--super or pension many on 'welfare payments'- etc-- Eg: I recently saw a video of small groups who <u>seemingly</u> — the video showed- Did live as *old style aboriginals* — with loin cloths and all covered in dust and mud — to live in old style homes or 'humpies' — fossicking for food- but alas- they were JUST operators who run "a holiday-- share the feeling group"--- who bring their paying guests — out in their 4wd vehicles then at end of "the tour" — they return them back to motels or hotels — with the required air-conditioned rooms-modern air-conditioned lounge and dining rooms — after which — all return to their city homes with their air-con--tv- where they can re-play videos of "their fantastic weekend off"-- to live in the bush — just as their ancestors had lived their lives.! But <u>in reality</u> — **it was just — A total fantasy- weekend**.! But when we look closer — there are many people around the country operating "guided day 4wd tours" —

Taking "tourists" on day/weekend Tours into 'the Outback' for Fees ranging from $150 to $389 per--to spend a day in- *"the life- of the aboriginals"*--most of who were born and live in the city—and just take these tourists out into the selected areas to teach them *"the way of life of aboriginals"*-- then go back home in their 4 wheel drive people carriers- because the dream of city living aboriginals have of "going-- **back to our culture"** — to live- be apart from 'civilisation' with its modern cons—their Ipad- TV or computers- certainly without food suppliers- drinks or alcohol- processed food- pizzas and McDonald's—when all combined there is no way they are ever likely to be going--**back to Our culture**— where they will all be called on- to hunt or seek food to eat— drink Rainwater-then, well-- most just couldn't survive-- only the younger aboriginals could ever survive—but 'the novelty' would soon wear off without their welfare payments and easy food options lost in such a total change.!
So- in my opinion—
This *'back to our culture'* idea-- is **a totally "factious" notion.**
Now--
before we move back to my story--I want to point something out- about the "numbers"- as:--
One report claimed--there were 260,000 aboriginals here-- prior to **"the invasion"** (that never happened.) One said-- there were 375,000 aboriginals here--then-another wrote there were 750,000 aboriginals—made up of 200 tribes.
Yes-- *not much difference*--*I do realise* —and particularly when none of them would have any way of ever knowing exactly what "the correct number" could have been.!
I--as anyone else- could not know exactly how or where these numbers came from--but--what this shows is—that-- N0 **No One really knew**--how many natives were here- just as No Other Country- knew there were humans living on--

This land — was why it was listed on charts as "terra nullius"-or- *Land belonging to no one* — Today some museums still show "terra australis" on the maps. A later report said-- largest portion of natives were in the gulf of Carpentaria-- So--if we say **475,000** natives were here x say 40%= 190,000- Est. lived in the gulf area with est. 80 tribes in that area -- then est. 60%= 285,000 were spread over other 120 tribes — which could mean within 'Sydney' area--there would likely have been just 2,375 aboriginals--in this general area--

The interesting thing here is--that it wasn't until Captain Phillip had befriended Colby- Bennelong and his friend- Yemmerrawanne — and was teaching them to read & write- as- he too was learning about their aboriginal language- and customs — that he was then to learn-- there **were many other 'natives'** actually living in other parts of this land — because Capt. Phillip had not left the general area of the colony — and even when food ships had not arrived — he had contracted with Pemulwuy to supply some meat for the colony.

So- it wasn't till long after Capt. Phillip had gone back to England that then exploration of the outer areas of NSW and Queensland- they discovered--the tribes mentioned- which could mean there had been 8,625 as being within New South Wales.!

If we were to accept the logic that- as-"the activist" reports say-there were- 300 massacred here--300 there — 'a thousand' massacred at waterloo creek and "thousands" died from disease and that the soldiers (who weren't there.) Massacred "20,000" etc. Even with NO bodies found etc.

The younger aboriginals still believe that there truly were thousands of their ancestors massacred in the Sydney area — which Logically would just not have been possible- because the-**net result-was** that None of the "activists" ever seem to-- consider or realise that the numbers they claim as —

237

Were- being massacred — When we ADD them all up — It would then have meant- **there were NO aboriginals left in the NSW part of Australia — by 1880.!?**
Due possibly- to the stability of food supply in the gulf of — Carpentaria area — the need to help 'the natives' was not so demanding — then being the furthest away from Sydney area maybe meant there was no attempt to 'develop' there — till later because there were No reports of Massacres found within that area- at all.! Still- with the hundreds of thousands as are claimed killed — by the British-to even use the 750,000 Total--as one claimed-- this would still mean — there would have been **NONE — Nil--Zippo** aboriginal/natives left — **by mid-** to late 1880's.!
So — To the aboriginals of today- I say again- whatever that you **"think you know"**- is only what you were *Told-- by those- "truth telling elders"-* which they most likely learnt from Their "Elders" coming to them in Their *"dream time stories-* which my research has proven are- and always have been--**the most "un- Likely to ever be Truthful"** Stories-- Yet such a very powerful source of information--you could ever imagine the next generations receiving.? So- I say To Dizzie and others:-- it may be best--**to focus:-- On what I write herein-** because the real answers — are within My Pages here and --I found answers different to as many of you are likely expecting — or would ever agree as being correct.!
Confirming — my whole theme then--is--
'the power of truth-telling — **will**--*realise change'.*
When I read "Dizzie" was saying:--
" I just wish people would listen and learn".?
Here I say--now--is a good time to "listen and learn"-- A good time-- "to read all of this book" — again- and again.! Where first I do point out- I write- with due-respects — and without prejudice to say — I see- most angst and calls —

For Retribution from colonisation of botany bay — and The wilful way settlers fenced off areas formerly used by The Aboriginals — the deaths-- all things-- as could be argued like forever — without any realistic conclusion being reached — but- be it that- <u>if we accept that</u> all claims were true then-- <u>We must also accept</u> the fact that **"the British"** and allies many decades later — did actually--

<u>SAVE</u> --the aboriginal race--IN The Darwin War —

Did SAVE The Aboriginals <u>*from extinction*</u> by the Japanese army invasion--**in 1942.!**
So — I say — can't- have one and not the other — then to me —
The Logic says — **we must be even**.!
So then--IF <u>the only way forward</u> will be to agree- Then--
"We" The **96.7%**-- will accept The early Illogical claims are correct — Then **"<u>You/the aboriginals</u>" must** <u>accept</u> that it was **Our Combined army as** *SAVED* the aboriginal race —
Saved them <u>from extinction</u>- by the Japanese army in 1942 — Which should then mean: — **we are even**--

We are even — then <u>together</u>--**we start again.!**
I therein do present this proposal as something no one else-- has ever done before-- <u>at least</u> — not--in an "<u>un-bias</u>" way as I Do see:-- because my sums featured on page 20/286--

Herein Say:-- **we should be equal.!**
And-I say- enough is enough.!

Let's Start Again.!

Australian pre-history
who-- was really here first.?

So- WHO FOUND Australia FIRST--
Who were "the discoverers" of Australia?

Records show--that in the **1420s** Australia's west and east coasts were visited and charted by **the Chinese--**
In fact- in a surge of navigation and discovery-
The Chinese mapped much of the world in 1420s.

The first of 29 Dutch voyages to Australia was in 1606-- While indigenous Australians claim to have inhabited the continent for 55,000 years, have traded with nearby islanders- The first documented landing--on--Australia by a European-- was in **1606**. There are few details of where the Dutch explorer Willem Janszoon landed on the western side of cape York peninsula and charted about 300 km of coastline — it is not known what happened there.!? **The idea that Captain Cook** discovered Australia was long debunked and was debated as recently as 2017 when <u>indigenous broadcaster Stan Grant</u> pointed to an inscription on his (cooks) statue in Sydney's Hyde park--the inscription reads –

"Discovered this territory 1770.".!
Robert Blyth, senior curator at the British maritime museum, said " it was not just the omission of existence of indigenous people that made this wrong- obviously there were indigenous Australians already there,"-Dr Blyth said-- "of course- other Europeans had encountered, had charted, had visited parts of Australia. The first European record of setting foot on- Australia was Dutch navigator Willem Janszoon in — 1606. The name **Australia** was popularised by Matthew Flinders following his circumnavigation of the continent in 1803. Australian explorer, Matthew Flinders, circa 1814.*(Wikimedia commons)* .Not only did Cook **not** claim he had discovered Australia--he wrote at the time, that he was destined for new holland. The main reason for his first voyage to the pacific was to observe **Venus** moving across the face of the sun from **Tahiti**-- "it was part of a European effort to work out the size of the solar system," Dr Blyth said. It was in Tahiti that he was to open an envelope with secret orders to search for an unknown continent.

The order was for him to try to discover the existence of 'terra australis incognita' — in other words, the 'great unknown southern land'," Dr Blyth said-- but—an aboriginal comment-- says-- **the aboriginals--did not accept that 'the British'**-- coming here in 1788- would Help them--so they rebelled--they fought - with spears and boomerangs--against guns and-- bayonets to-**get rid of 'the British'**-

How quaint- and how-- so-totally in-correct — and obviously written by an aboriginal after 2010.! Because this totally contradicts Capt. Phillips journals — and the British 'guns' were in very short supply- so this remark was obviously written by some "activists" like 200+ years Later by someone who had NO idea of what they were writing about —

Someone who had-- <u>Not</u> read the journals.! Which Said:-
At the colony—Even in the first months—the natives could
See all the new Tents- then Buildings started and could see
development in food supply-with crops sown--and Capt.
Phillip set up "a Govt. System"--to control things--to help
everyone. Yes--there were 4 aboriginal deaths--but no more in
Capt. Phillips time-till **Pemulwuy** -because he did believe--*it
is not acceptable to kill another human being* — but later the
retribution sometimes could have been strong as most of the
whites that were killed were un-armed-- because in general
the convicts and the settlers did not have guns--
<u>My research showed</u>- that if the mariners were called out--
It was **to retaliate** for a white being killed or for some serious
theft of stock or wheat- food-- etc.?
Yet-- today--the aboriginal 'Activists'--**only see** what *they say*
happened to **their ancestors**--*or- what they have been* **told** *by* --
"*the truth teller elders*"-what happened to them—they make *no
allowance* for the situation that most of the reports they relate
to--were--as I found- <u>usually</u> written very much later- by
aboriginals—then many decades later- on The Net—where at
least 2-3 versions of the reports-have been "made up"-as facts-
-often hard to decipher--often don't ever match.? **And—Now
some 230+ years later**—They still refuse to accept this—even
in spite of developments that 'the British' have made here--
with their attempts to educate--to rid tribes of in-breeding--
rape and sexual violence-to improve the country's defence
systems and create Food supply--but still "the elders" refuse
to see/or admit any of this--still totally blaming "the
British"—for anything.! Still rebelling--still fighting-- to do--
what.? Wait **for the Japanese to come--again.?**
But-- I wonder--or *more to the point*--**I ask--**What do The
Activists- really want.?

They say they want to be known as "One Nation"- but—does it matter who really was here first.?
I Find NO—because They have been badly misled--

<u>To look back</u>-- at the land maps--such as those depicting 170 million years ago- as shown herein   there are several areas:-- where people could easily have found their way across land mass—to even have then walked into what we now call "Australia"-
To remember:--I wrote much of this section before the 2021 "Mungo man" DNA Bombshell.!

Yet--who could have imagined that:--

170 million years ago--

That People-- could just "hop/or flit" from One Land-mass--to another--

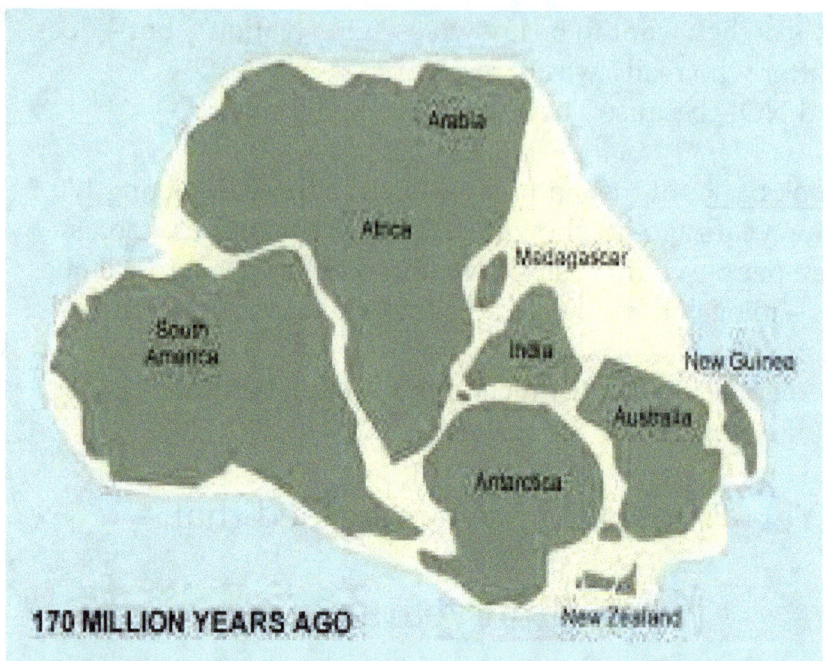

170 MILLION YEARS AGO

YES--this theory- is still supported when looking at the maps in the next pages also--which shows the period of some-even then--**80 million years ago**--it is reported on one—'**Earliest Australians'** web pages--that the aboriginal movement from Africa--to Australia did culminate in a series of hazardous sea voyages across island southeast Asia—yet earlier reports said that in "fact" **70,000** years ago people actually **'walked'** across the land mass from- as is now called Papua new guinea--the word 'Papua' is said to be derived from local folklore meaning -"of un-certain origin"--and then could put strength to the earlier historical maps which show **70,000** years ago these countries were all still melded tight together—But within- 'the ice age' had been gradually breaking apart- then around **50,000** years ago to become--the individual islands we know today. That also tends to make sense of reports that show—

The 'moving' Plates of earth's surface as do-- Surround Our Australia- Recent studies suggest the last voyage, potentially between Timor/Roti and the northern Kimberley coast, would have involved advanced planning skills, four to seven days of hard paddling on a raft, for a total group of more than 100 to 400 people. Yet aboriginal "Myth" believes some thousands of aboriginals were here 50,000 years ago.! The possibility that earlier waves of modern human populations might have moved out of Africa before 50,000 years has also been raised.
But in a review of these events, it points out that there is **No convincing fossil evidence** to support this idea beyond-- the middle east.
One of the most important claimed potential early sites is in northern Australia, at **Madjedbebe, rock** shelter in Arnhem land. Human presence here was recently declared--at more than 65,000 years ago--which again tends to confuse "Facts".!
This 65,000 year- date has rapidly become accepted as the age for colonisation of Australia--yet none have stated--where they did believe the people actually came from.!
And so--I ask--IF aboriginals came 55,000 years ago- then-who were the people here before – what happened to them.?
Were 'they' here to greet aboriginals-were they friendly or hostile.? The discovery of *"mungo lady"* and *"mungo man"* said to have died in Australia--62,000 years ago--pose many questions--
But then: Scientists- Alan Coper, Alan n. Williams and Nigel Spooner--say: *aboriginal Australians have effectively been on their country as long as modern human populations have been outside of Africa. Our review of the scientific evidence published today in proceedings of the national academy of sciences – suggests that – for all practical purposes, this is indeed the case. Their ancestors arrived shortly after 50,000 years ago– effectively forever, given that modern human populations only moved out of Africa 50,000- to--*

246

*55,000 years ago. It was only a few thousand years earlier that a --
Small population of modern humans moved out of Africa.
As they did, they met and briefly hybridised with neandertals before rapidly spreading around the world.
They became the genetic ancestors of all surviving modern human populations outside of Africa--who are all characterised by a distinctive small subset of neandertal DNA around 2.5% preserved in their genomes- this distinctive marker is found in aboriginal population indicating they are part of this original diaspora, but one that must have moved to Australia almost immediately after-leaving Africa--nevertheless, this myth is pervasive, even though there is insufficient historical or scientific proof, and some state this is because the myth is politically useful. (6).*
Writer 'Claire Coleman' also on aboriginal web page. Notes *"this argument leads inevitably, unless it had started that way, to the statement that the English were merely **the most recent** arrivals of **multiple overlapping invasions**." And- "aboriginal people are not deserving of land-rights because **we** invaded someone else":-- "the people here before are the one's deserving of land rights, but they are all dead. As such, we all become 'invaders'; **there are No 'First peoples' alive**, only second and third-wave Australians.*

> *And therefore, the pygmy myth can be used as a way to justify the ongoing invasion of first nations lands by stating that **the British** were just stealing land that **first nations** people Stole"--*
> *"this could be why the myth not only exists in Australia; there are similar myths existing in other colonised countries as well".*
> Reports however *tend to expand upon this information as it says that somewhere around* **70,000** *years ago-- people had migrated from parts of Asia--into the top or northern end — of Australia-which happened to be some 20,000 years* **before** *"the aboriginals" came to Australia* **55,000 years** *ago-- which surely creates doubts to the claim that the aboriginals-- were* **"the First Australians".?**

It confirms why--in recent years--they have changed "their title" to now be known differently- to be as-"**the custodians**" of the land.? Then reports appeared widely in the media and elsewhere within political statements and comments by the Prime Minister of that decade--which poses **more confusion** as--why are our governments of 2010 on--All co-towing to the aboriginal groups of today — as They are First Nation People.?
Because there is good reason to question a **55,000**-year date, and the extent to which this contrasts with the sudden wave of some of the archaeological sites that swept across Australia shortly after 50,000 years ago.
These sites include Barrow island and Carpenters gap in the Kimberley's- Devils lair south of Perth, Willandra lakes in-- NSW and- Warratyi - rock shelter- in the flinders ranges. This rapid archaeological manifestation at 50,000 years is a perfect match for the genetic evidence from aboriginal maternal, paternal, and genomic lineages, and a far better fit-- with the extinction of Australia's megafauna around 42,000 years ago. **Re- An age limit for human migration--**one of the most interesting ways we can date the dispersal of modern humans around the globe, including Australia, is through-- That original interbreeding event with neandertals as they left Africa. About a decade ago, an ancient human leg bone was found on the banks of a Siberian river by an ivory hunter. Radiocarbon-dated it at 43,000-45,000 years ago, the entire genome of this individual, named Ust'-Ishim after the site, was sequenced using the latest ancient DNA technology. The genomic sequence revealed the bone contained the standard 2.5% neandertal DNA signal carried by all non-Africans. But it was still present in large continuous blocks and had yet not been dispersed into fragments around the genome as we see in more recent ancestors and ourselves.

In fact, the size of the blocks showed that the 43,000-45,000-year-old Ust'-Ishim specimen could only be a maximum of--230-430 generations after the initial neandertal liaison— Dating movement out of Africa to no more than 50,000-55,000 years ago--**or no more than 65,000 years?**

Given the evidence is so strong that the ancestors of modern human populations only started moving around the world 50,000-55,000 years ago, could the human activity then at--Madjedbebe really be more than **65,000** years old?

Is the question--one of the major limitations of **Modderbee** is that the stone artefacts themselves weren't dated, just the surrounding sand layers. As a result, over time, even the slightest downward movement of the artefacts within the unconsolidated sand layers at Madjedbebe would make them appear too old.

We Identify a range of factors which are common around the site, such as termite burrowing and heavy rainfall, that could cause stone artefacts to sink.

Many archaeological signs suggest activity at Madjedbebe is actually much younger than **65,000** years, and overall, the extent to which the site is an outlier to the rest of the Australian record should raise a red flag.

Connection to country--either way, aboriginal Australians Believe they have effectively been on their country as long as modern human populations have been outside of Africa.

Dr Graham Brown, a research associate from the museum and art gallery of the northern territory, was a contributor on this article.!

THEN- we look into the 'Ice Age'-- where-to look--and see who- could have first come here into Australia—there does still appear several "other options".!

In guise to create 'awareness' of — *the aboriginal or indigenous people* as being--"the First Australians"--or- "Custodians" of-

The land- today -**IF--<u>anyone cared to look</u> "back"--then--
history shows** There are likely <u>many</u> other options—
Because--it shows Australia was still connected to all of those
Countries—
So there could easily have been "others" here first-- **that is--
if anyone**—did-- <u>Care to</u> look:--
The Ice Age continues the story--

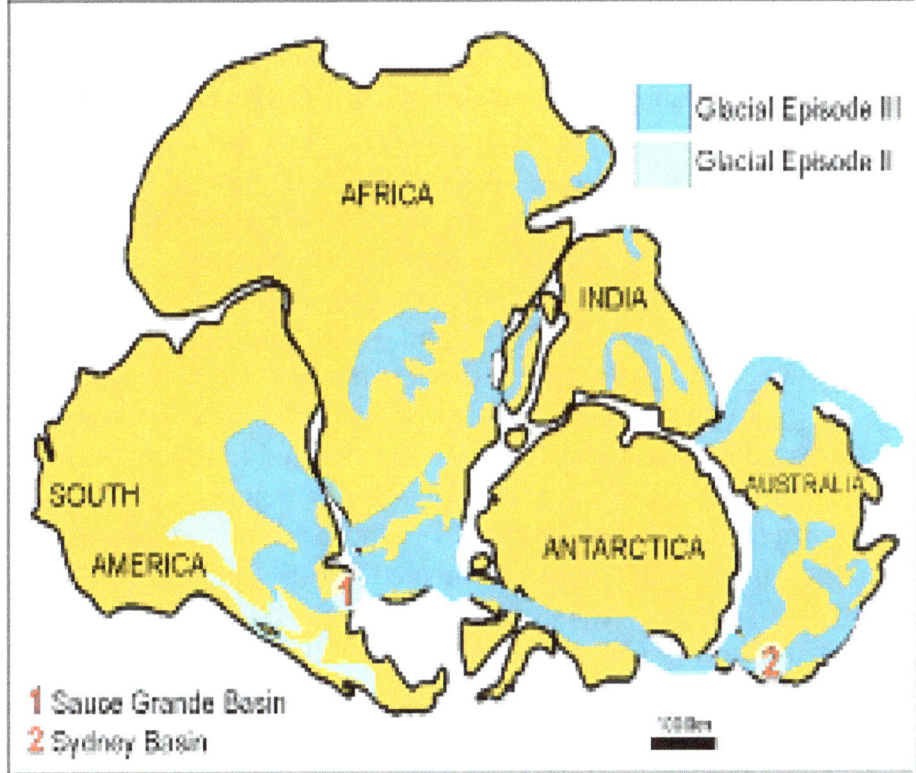

On one side-- today--we have these 'Facts'--then--
I am seeing--on <u>another side</u>- it then grows--keeps growing
so strongly with current **internet** and other media statements
and discussions--even openly at public functions—where--
'the writer' of such contentious articles are just **never
checked**-or--even questioned--never asked for their 'Proof'--
Or--asked for 'Evidence' etc-

250

All being totally distorted as in many years of research- and--
with such personal experiences-- I have found that these
'Activists and reporters'-- as others--are writing their stories-
and are all claiming them to be **'Facts'** when they are **mostly
"made-up"-** _personal_- **"Facts".!**
So then-- who did find the land first-**?**
Yes- who did.? Really is-- the $64 question.?
We have lots of confusion--a myriad of--_personal_ "made-up"--
"_facts_"- I found it common "the ancestors"- really becomes
accepted their decendants are of--**"the first Australians"--**
not even thinking/or caring about the fact that "their-so
called--first australians"--were extremely vunerable- wide
open to some foreign country to invade this country. To
invade and—as was the German's plan--to **totally Wipe--
'The Jews' Right out—Germany could easily have become
an early Invader—of This Land—as others--**if the reviled
"1788 British Invaders" had not come here **first.!**
In the main I am amazed the _"misguided" and "misrepresented"_
Obsessed young aboriginals--are being led in the main over--
so many decades- and centuries- of such 'made-up'--
"_dream time stories_" coming from those who _they believe_ are—
their most 'trusted' and 'respected' "truth telling elders"--
not suspecting—not ever thinking that:--their--
"**truth telling elders" have been--leading them astray.?**
As we now have learnt that their "original" owners—had--
known from way back—that **"the mungo clan"—**
were here before their ancestors-- not suspecting that:-
they maybe were likely --being conned.**!**
The _confirmation of bias_ refers to a psychological tendency of
people to ignore any facts that undermine preconceived
notions of the world. Perhaps a good example of the bias at
work is the manner that Australian prehistory has—

Largely been ignored — because it throws up countless mysteries-- That are inconsistent with traditional theories of Australian and world evolution- Finding mungo lady-then— The mungo man put a spanner in the works of traditional theories--but few acknowledged "mango lady" the first being found in " broken format"--till then a few years later "mungo man" was found in a complete format—"**Mungo man**" was a hominin with a fine skeleton like modern humans who was estimated to have died **62,000 years ago**. The ANU'S John Curtin school of medical research found that mungo man's skeleton's- contained a small section of mitochondrial DNA. After analysing the DNA, the school found that mungo man's DNA bore no similarity to other ancient skeletons, or-- to modern aborigines as modern Europeans--
Which were then Locked away in A University because this was **not politically appropriate.!**
Furthermore, his mitochondrial DNA-- had become extinct. The results called into question the 'out of Africa' theory of human evolution. If mungo man was descended from a person who had left Africa in the past 200,000 years, then his mitochondrial DNA should have looked like all of the other samples--but the experts said it did not.!
Opportunism well alive: --
I note-- on one "aboriginal" web page — it invites visitors to-- *come visit the "mungo national park"* — *learn of* ***mungo lady*** *and* ***mungo man*** *part of an ancient culture dating back where mungo man was a part of their "ritual burials"* **42,000 years ago** — *and they say--descendants of the couple--still do live in the area-to-this day.! (no names or pics.?) I Say- that seems* **highly unlikely**.! My research found — IF mungo lady and **mungo man** died — here **62,000 years ago**- as first reported--then it is most likely that he was purposefully buried in--some form of "rock grave"- to be preserved--to be kept intact for some future--

252

Generations to find--<u>to prove</u> that there **was a-- Human Race right** Here--on the land that we now call "Australia" — long before the aboriginals.!

Then--the aboriginals in promoting to claim the **mungo man/lady** people had died "<u>over</u> 42,000 years ago"-- **is a great way** to get visitors to come to Mungo park —

Which again — is adding to the **confusion-** *because this claim--* I say- we can't prove them wrong—just as they can't prove they are right-- either — so this is pushing boundaries of false or misleading advertising- 'legally' because "experts" have reported-they were found and adjudged to have died **62,000 years ago**--therein — naturally then being the humans here in that century--which then has proven that their race--had really existed.

Then any of the others- as these people-who make other claims--were doing so- to suit their own needs--or benefit-- another "false- *or made-up* story". Another spanner in the traditional aboriginal theories were the **Kow swamp** skeletons from Northern Victoria, which were reminiscent of homo erectus. Specifically, they had thick brow ridges, and-sloping foreheads--and very large teeth. If <u>Kow swamp</u> skeletons had been found in Indonesia and dated at **100,000 + years ago**--then they might have been categorised as homo erectus-- but being *found in Australia* dated at only 10,000 years- it **was problematic**.

According to traditional theories, homo erectus never reached Australia and was believed to have died out when the homo sapiens reached Indonesia in excess of 50,000 years ago. Even if the <u>Kow swamp</u> people weren't homo erectus, it was hard to explain why — an ancient looking people occupied Australia *after* a more modern looking people had been in Australia. This specimen and others from the middle east are the oldest known traces of modern humans outside-

Of Africa. They prove that homo sapiens had started to--
Spread out of --Africa by 100,000 years ago, although it may
be that these remains represent a population that did not--
Expand beyond this region – with migrations to the rest of
the world likely occurring later, about 60-70,000 years
ago. Evolved in it did belong to as homo sapiens.
While **mungo man** and the Kow swamp skeleton undermine
theories of the biological evolution of humanity,
The Bradshaw paintings (Gwion Gwion) undermine theories
of cultural evolution. A fossilised wasp nest covering one of
the paintings has been dated at 17,000+ years old, which is
highly problematic, because the art is unlike palaeolithic art--
When found elsewhere in the world — specifically--
paleolithic art typically uses animals as the primary subject
while the Bradshaw's typically depict humans. In addition,
the Bradshaw's show the humans with tassels, hair
adornments, and possibly clothing.
Such body adornments are usually found in agricultural
societies that have developed hierarchical systems of status.
In a nutshell, the art shows cultural approaches that were not
believed to exist until agriculture developed around 10,000
years ago. Aside from being problematic--because of the
signs of an agricultural culture 10,000 years before
agriculture developed anywhere in the world — and on a
continent where agriculture was not believed to have been
developed-- until the arrival of Europeans- the art is
problematic because of some of the technology and animals
portrayed. For example:- *one cave painting shows a line of deer,*
which is surprising- when considering there is no evidence of
deer ever existing within Australia-- prior to the arrival of
Europeans. Another painting of a boat seems to show a
rudder, a keel-- and a design typically fashioned using metal
tools; however, at 17,000+ years old, such a boat would--

Predate development of such technology x 15,000 Yrs. The prevalence of migrant flora and fauna that arrived prior to Europeans also undermines conceptions that Australia--Fauna and flora owed their uniqueness to geographic isolation. The migrant flora includes the Boab tree and--Kangaroo grass, which are native to Africa. The migrant Fauna includes the keelback snake, bogal, water rat and dingo that had ancestral origins in Asia. The lengthy flow of flora and fauna back and forth between Australia and other countries pose some questions about why some species took hold but some did not.

For example, if humans brought Dogs with them in their canoes from India, why didn't they bring pigs when walking overland from Papua new guinea? Likewise, if the boab tree and kangaroo grass could reach Australia from Africa, why couldn't Rice reach Australia--from Asia or sweet potato from Papua new guinea?

For those people who seek the certainty of agreement, the mysteries of Australian prehistory are highly threatening because they undermine what we have been taught and any possible answers they develop are unlikely to unite audiences in consensus. For those driven by curiosity however, mysteries of Australian prehistory provide countless opportunities -- to see The World anew.

Alan cooper, director, Australian centre for ancient DNA University of Adelaide; Alan n Williams, Assn. Investigator, ARC centre of excellence for Australian biodiversity + heritage unsaw, and Nigel Spooner, adjunct professor, university of Adelaide says this article originally to publish on the conversation. It read as the original article.

*Some anthropologists have suggested different cultures once existed in the **Kimberley** as in the study referred to here. Nobody knows for sure when people who painted this unique rock art first arrived.*

255

The oldest known human remains found in Australia, **mungo man,** *were* **found not to be related** *to* modern day aborigines*-- In at least one study. Of course- people disagree with this, which once again proves Senator Leyonhjelm's main point as manifestly true--the senator is not expressing an opinion one way or the other, Except that-- anthropologists do debate these things.*
At the time, there was controversy about their origins but not over the fact of their existence. In 1962, the first volume of Manning Clark's *history of Australia* recorded-their presence on its first two pages and repeated the then influential-- anthropological theory about their origins — and their place in the waves of migration-of hunter-gatherer peoples from Asia who populated the Australian continent in the millennia before the British arrived in 1788.
Yet, since then, the Australian pygmies have been totally obliterated from public memory. To test just how complete this process has been, over recent months we have questioned a wide range of friends and acquaintances. Although most were well-educated and well-read people, none had ever heard of The Pygmies, not even when we used some of their other, once-familiar alternative names such as "Neuritis" and then the "Barrineans". A few friends scoffed at the notion- demanded some evidence.
They wouldn't believe until we email them photographs. The *encyclopedia of aboriginal Australia* (1994), published by the Australian institute of aboriginal and Torres strait islander studies, today does its best to disguise these people.
It lists some of their tribes, including the Djabuganjdji, Mbarbaram (Barbaram) and Yidinjdji (Indindji), but does not mention a word about their stature.
Only its entry of "rainforest".? Another map shows--at least 65,000 years ago there was archaeological evidence of-- The first people on the Australian continent--

256

Two widely accepted possible routes used by the first people to reach Australia identified by Joseph Birdsell in 1977 – Were-Researched by the Australian national university- which show the red northern route as more likely as used –

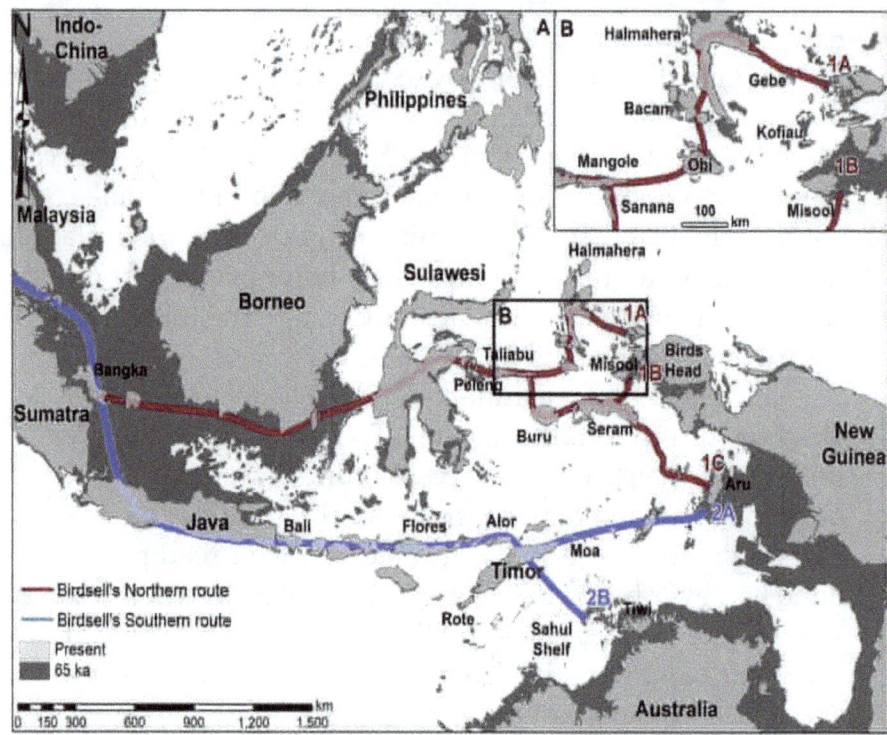

Photograph: supplied by Shimona Kealy/ANU.
Wed 31 oct 2018 04.00 aedt-- details on this may show the first people to arrive in Australia are likely to have sailed east from Borneo to Sulawesi- island hopped to New guinea, according to research. A study led by Australian national university PhD candidate **Shimona Kealy** and published in the journal of human evolution has modelled the most likely route from southeast Asia to the Australian mainland based on-- which pathway would have required the least expenditure of energy and resources.

257

Kealy said *she hoped the research would help answer the question of why archaeological sites in Australia--which show human-- occupation around 65,000 years ago are so much older than sites- That have been discovered in the countries that were long suspected To be en-route. Her modelling identified the least-cost route as going from Borneo to Sulawesi and through a series of smaller — Islands-- to Misool island off the coast of west Papua new guinea was connected by land to Australia until about 10,000 years ago, meaning the first people could walk down through what is now Cape York to the rest of the continent.*

"The visibility and the shorter distances between the islands is what really makes this route much more feasible for travel." She told Guardian Australia. "most of the time that visibility is shore-to-shore visibility."

Kealy also tracked other factors, like whether a particular route would involve going over or around a hill, in order to determine the most likely path of travel. "we are looking at the first sea journey of our species," she said. The route follows roughly the same path as the northern route described by US anthropologist joseph Birdsell in 1977, who theorised two likely paths to have been largely accepted as used as model for researchers.

Birdsell's *northern route goes through Sulawesi to west Papua and the southern route goes through Timor and ends with a significant sea crossing to the northern territory or-- Kimberley-coastline. Archaeologists-have since found a number of sites in east Timor that show proof of human occupation, but none are older than 45,000 years old.* **Artefacts** *from oldest known site in Australia, are a rock shelter at Madjedbebe in the Jabiluka mining lease within Kakadu national park, on Marrar country have been dated as **65,000** year old A site on Barrow island off the coast of western Australia -- "obviously people had to travel through these islands somehow to get to Australia-- so presumably the dates – that we found in Australia should be younger or around the same age as the dates that we are getting from these east Timor sites--*

<u>Kealy said</u>. *The fact that those sites are significantly younger, suggests that maybe the First Peoples took a different path. The islands -on Birdsell's northern route- received comparatively Little archaeological attention due to isolation, expense, and political conflict in west Papua.*
Kealy + co-author <u>Prof sue</u> <u>O'Connor</u> are applying for some- Research grants to investigate some likely sites along the northern route next year. She said,
"If we <u>can</u> find something that's older than 60,000 years old-- I would be super-dooper happy," <u>she said</u>.
The timeframe of **65,000 plus** years is not universally accepted in the academic community.   Another recent study asserted 50,000 to 55,000 years was the most likely timeframe — but-- Kealy said *her modelling tracked changes in both coastline and sea level from 45,000 to **70,000** years ago. The sea level was at its lowest point **65,000 years** ago and highest 70,000 years ago.*
So still the aboriginal birthplace--**is a mystery**--and then without anything such as that--they-(the aboriginees)-- **Can't prove** their lineage--equally though-- <u>as I said before</u>- it also means--**none can prove** them wrong <u>either</u>.!
Simply/logically the internet creators of today have now compiled most information passed on in their *"<u>dream time stories</u>"*-- or — their own *"<u>made-up</u>"* versions of these-- *"<u>dream time stories</u>"*.! Because--there is **No written** coverage of any events from before or around 50,000 years ago. No reports that can be classed as being created by <u>independent</u> reporters--but one by one- these reports of lineage--turn out to be mainly written by *"aboriginal people"* wishing to "prove a point" — <u>I found</u>--taking any opportunity to 'push a barrow'- play politics- believing — if- its written-then others think its correct and so they will be right- believing Others will read it — then think it must be true.!

Why else would it be written--but for all to read.?
Why else--indeed.?
All of these people overlook **the one true fact**--being that--
Amazingly-from **170 million years ago**--down through--
"the ice age"- **80 million years ago**--
This country--which "the English" settlers finally named
"Australia"--was joined to — Or in close proximity to
Antarctica, New Zealand, Asia-- Sth. America, and
Madagascar-- forming the last remnant of--the great
southern landmass called "**Gondwana**"--
So- **early people** could have come from any of those
countries-- or--from all of them.!
    * about 80 million years ago new Zealand started to
      Drift away from the rest of Gondwana...
    * Australia was joined to southeast Asia, new Zealand,
      Antarctica, and south America, forming the last
      remnant of the great southern landmass called-
      Gondwana.
    * the Australian part of Gondwana was located close
      to the south pole.
    * Southern Australia- lay within the Antarctic circle-
      Reports say "aboriginals" came in boats —
They also say that 50,000 years ago--thousands of people
walked into the top end of Australia.
But--what happened between **80 million** years ago and--
then--**60,000** years ago — is not clear as--<u>there are no records</u>.!
There are no Facts-- nor information to show--**where the
original owners did--come from--**and-
were they still here-- when the Aboriginals arrived.?
What happened to them.?
    What **did they die--**<u>what from</u>.?
    Or-- where they killed.?
    If so — how were they Killed.? — and **BY whom.?**

SO- my queries about the aboriginal "made up facts"-- **are many**-- yet aboriginals who do know--ignore history that is Real and True --and do Not pass on--these **true stories--they only pass on Own** *"made up"* *"dream time stories".!* To me-- I say — it doesn't matter a rats ass- what matters is that **"the elders" I suggest--**
Have always denied their kin — **"the truth"--** and instead have passed on their *"made-up stories"* of vitrol- and they still--***won't accept*** what--"the british" wanted to do — nor what-- they really have done-for- **the aboriginal race**--in Australia--Yet--*ironically* they never "Regress" from what- **they say--**happened at Sites as Waterloo creek on the-- 26/1/1886--and--it is the *"un-proven-truths"*-- they did pass on in their strong *"brainwashing routines"*- *as* they continually tell — Their young Generations that--Waterloo creek"- was--

The worst "massacre" in aboriginal history. —
           when they know this is "a Furphy".!
I say again "a Furphy"--**to be sure we have got it right.!**

Then maybe it's about time — that we learnt the Real Truth —
behind the — To ME-- 'in-famous' professor Lyndall Ryan's
Magic — *"massacres map"* — and why it was commissioned.?
Maybe we should ask — hey- Ms professor Ryan-- WHO Did
Commission and Approve **Subsidy $$s** to create 'The Map'.?

AND- Did you/and They also-know about "the mango's"?

So here now--I am "changing direction"--
but- I must first say--that after having found such incredible
news--I do also believe that way back- for "the elders" to
have **decided** to use **"brainwashing"** techniques **in their**
"dream-time stories" to control all future generations
"thinking"--in fact — to be guiding their lives —

This was incredibly Clever--
This was the most **ingenious** *plan--* that "the elders" from way
back est 200+ years ago — Did create — Then have made sure
that "The elders" of each generations -had used The Same
Plans To "keep it going" right through to be controlling The
Total Aboriginal Race today.!
So--Here I wright This history using — 'aboriginal' web sites
"theme"-- **'the power of *truth-telling* to realise change'**
This 'action line' — helped me-*'re- wright history'* — in--

"Kevs wake up Australia."

AND--In conclusion-- I say-- to all — we have Both gained Huge Losses — CAN'T Claim One — without Accepting the Other-- SO I SAY:-- WE should be equal —
Should Be as ONE Multi-cultural Country.!

We can't change the past...

But — it's time-- to change direction for Future--

<u>it's time--</u> to wake up--

Because--I 'see'- a <u>racist</u> disaster looming.?

we all should **celebrate**:--
Australia day + a Darwin war day.

HERE:--I now must close:-- but wait —

Confusion — still reigns supreme as: —
One University- has said the DNA — was not--
 Same as aboriginal--
But-- recently- another university says 'their'--
U-Beaut-DNA test process says first DNA <u>is wrong</u>
It Was aboriginal DNA--
<u>Then recently</u>--
as I checked photos of the Mungo burial sites —
showing how they were buried, and where they
were Buried — then tried to find reports *(not written by aboriginals)* as showed that--

<u>The Willandra lakes area</u>- where the mungo's were found — A Report Shows from 32 million thru to 6 million then to 150,000 years ago — It Said--

Each period-- had deposited a layer of silt/dirt over the area — and — IT Says:--
The Lunettes that the mungo's were found in-- were more like *the cremation style and burial of* **another race** —

As these Lunettes were not consistent with the known aboriginal burial ritual sites —
Yet aboriginals of the area-- are positive that-- *the **mungo's**--* <u>were aboriginals</u>.?

So--Oh boy--this story--
    May not be at its end-- just yet.?

    So — I Say — **"watch this space"**--

This "My Aboriginal Story" May Not be at an End-

There could very well be —

    more to come.?

author

aussiekevG.

Weapons and
THE WARS

IN This part--
I relate — briefly to **The Wars that "Australia"- Did Fight IN —** To Say —

THIS IS All Part of OUR History

I SAY Briefly:-- That In my search of 'the internet' — I found there are many entries and information of and about those wars and the australians- including aboriginals- who had fought with such allies- to also learn that--

Each time--many aboriginals had volunteered — and had fought side by side with our multi-nation Aussies where all were just Australians-- Fighting to help our Allies — in hope that one day — IF we ever needed them — they would come to help us-
Which was not required — till 1942 — when the Japanese Army did try to invade Australia — via Darwin.

Here — I point out-- that I have included some 'Copies' of photos and articles with the source on some--I have featured these because I believe that to create OUR Australian History To teach our children--the history of our multi-cultural Australia — then — these people and their stories with Old photos--are what should become a big part of OUR History — because if these people had not been here — then-- this generation of Aussie's- incl. Aboriginals-- **would not be here--TODAY.!**
I say:--forget about "made-up" stories of aboriginals and The "Massacres or Slaughters" which most likely did not happen- As no bodies were ever found —

BUT Here- with-- 'The wars' we know who fought and who died — It's all on Record.!

And I say:--it's way beyond time--to include them-- in **OUR Australian history.!**

First — I see--there were 'the wars' where australia did fight to Help our 'Allies'--to help stall any agressor--who- might have later-- come to our Australian shores- starting with-- **the Boer war-**

We have fought together--as Australians —
Many aboriginals men & women volunteered--academics say many men did not identify themselves as indigenous or often used different names to enlist. Dr Kerwin says he believes there was also a small contingent of aboriginal men who served in the Boer war in 1902- and did not make it home. Only 12 men have been identified and were honoured as aboriginal Soldiers. Last week two more men were identified - Dale Kerwin from Griffith University said-- *I think it is likely- "those 50-- didn't want to come home".?* Didn't want to go back to "the elders" aboriginal way of life.!

The first Australian troops arrived in south Africa in December 1899, too late to become involved in the serious-- British defeats of "black week" (10-17 December), when 2,300 men were killed or wounded by the Boers in three separate-- engagements. Five hundred members of the Queensland Mounted Infantry and the NSW Lancers took part in the relief of Kimberley in February 1900, and men of the NSW Mounted Rifles played a minor part in the last major battle of the war, at Paardeberg, in the same month. After a series of defeats in 1900 the Boer armies quickly became fragmented, forming groups of highly mobile commandos which harassed British troop movements and lines of supply. Faced with this type of warfare, the British commanders became increasingly reliant on Mounted troops from Britain and The Colonies.   Conditions for both soldier and horse were harsh- with no time to acclimatise.

Now equally as I have been pointing out the weapons of choice of the aboriginal race--and the inability of these to be suited for anywhere else than as aboriginals use them to Hunt for food--

On checking out wars the Australian armed forces have fought in--partly to defend this country- which in turn would also be- *defending the lives of the aboriginal race* as well--mindful that I did point out that Captain Phillips said in no uncertain terms-IF they were called on to defend themselves--against a fully armed enemy--the whole aboriginal race--would have been annihilated — **completely wiped out.!**

Which also creates more questions as--why- aboriginals have continued to use their old weapons--

I really do wonder why.? And I have no valid answer.? As it now seems like so many aboriginals having been to war-have been trained to use modern weapons — many--

Obviously- one would assume--in early wars would have fired single shot Rifles and hand-guns- thrown grenades and likely used mortars even used machine guns.

Then--I must add- **thank Christ- that they did not**--but--as mentioned earlier--this then-- is quite a puzzle-- because most Aussie's would not relate to the fact that our Aboriginals--whilst most were still in such a *rebellious* mood here--with "activists" literally fighting everything the ruling government was trying to do--To Help them- yet--
I also was amazed to first learn that right from back to 1902 Boer war--then-<u>the Gallipoli campaign</u> in the first world war that took place on the Gallipoli peninsula, from 17 February 1915 to-- 9 January 1916. The entente powers, Britain, France- and Russia, sought to weaken "the Ottoman Empire"- one of the central powers, by taking control of the Turkish straits where Australia fought in Gallipoli?
The campaign began with a failed naval attack by British and French ships on the Dardanelles straits in February- March 1915 and--continued with a major land invasion of the Gallipoli peninsula on April 25, involving British and French Troops as well as division of the Australian and new Zealand army corps (Anzac).30 April-
Aboriginal peoples whose ancestors- had lived in Australia for thousands of years before Europeans arrived — Many did **volunteer** to help Fight. Aware of confrontations with "the settlers" as a result of the arrival of the British "First fleet" in 1788 in Australia- here--at this time- for many hundreds of young aboriginals to volunteer to join with Australia--to actually go away overseas — likely against "Elders" wishes-- To fight to try to protect Australia from any future likely invaders--to me was nothing less than **Incredible** —
And-- These 'Things' ARE what SHOULD become Part of **"OUR History"** —

In view of the fact--that most of the older--And those too young to fight--were still hell bent on rebelling-- against the government at Home-and any of its campaigns to try and Help the aboriginals'--
As to how--in view of so many of our aborigines having been to war--that they came home to once again use the old spears and boomerangs etc to Hunt for their Food-- after using other weapons of destruction- then to the latest who have shown just how much Australia going to war-- Did mean to these people--and-- the reasons why Australia has been going to war-- and fighting in so many wars--since settling in Botany Bay Australia in 1788.

First world war-- 4 august 1914 to 31 March 1918--

Over 1,000 aboriginal and Torres strait islander people served in world war 1 (1914-1918) and around 70 fought at Gallipoli.

Australia's involvement in the first world war began when Britain and Germany went to war on 4 august 1914-

Wikipedia result: ottoman victory ww1

At the outbreak of the war large numbers of Australians came forward to enlist, and aboriginal Australians also answered the call. Best current estimates are that about 1,000 indigenous Australians – out of an estimated population of 93,000 in 1901 fought in the first world war (though the real number is probably higher.). It is not known what motivated indigenous Australians to join Ihe Australian Imperial Force (AIF).

But loyalty and patriotism doubtless played a part. There was also the incentive of a receiving a wage. Indigenous soldiers were paid- the same rate as the non-indigenous soldiers.

In general--indigenous soldiers served under the same conditions of service as other members of the AIF, with many experiencing in the army- equal treatment for the first time in their lives.
There may have also been the hope that having served would deliver greater equality after the war.
In reality, however-- upon their return to civilian life they were treated with the same prejudice and discrimination as before they went to war- (*says an aboriginal reporting source.*).

Second world war 3 September 1939 to 30 June 1945

At least 3000 aboriginal and 850 Torres strait islander people served in world war ii (1939-1945)

The Korean war and the Vietnam war.
Australian forces also supported Britain in Malaya assisted against Indonesia.
Korean war, 1950–53.
In the early 20th century, as a federated dominion and later as an independent nation, Australia fought in the first world war and second world war, as well as in the wars in Korea, Malaya, Borneo- and Vietnam during the cold war...

IN total, nearly 103,000 Australians died during these conflicts.

second world war, 1939–45

As a member of the western alliance, Australia fought in two of the biggest conflicts of "the cold war"--

As World war 11 was ending, the cold war began-- this was to be a long lasting and continuing confrontation between--

The Soviet union and the United states, lasting from 1945 to 1989. It was called- The Cold War- because neither the soviet union nor the united states officially declared war on each other.

Over a million Australians — including many thousands of aboriginals-- served in the Second world war. They fought in campaigns against Germany and Italy in Europe, the-- Mediterranean and north Africa, as well as against Japan in south-east Asia and other parts of the pacific.
Both men and women, served in the second world war –
Now:--
<u>I am not a military expert</u>- *and I am just 'Presenting' This Information AS I have Found it – and I present this - aa a part of the Real Story for Experts to 'Follow through' to find The Words and Photos as are relevant – as They SHOULD Be Included as A Part of OUR History – I Do Not understand Why such Stories are Not already Presented in Our History to our School children--*
But- to me-- in general it seems to be-- *that if we could ever need to call for assistance from another country--to repel any attack or attempts to invade our country--then we need to have relationships with other nations as we would call "an Ally"---*

By first fighting with them--so that if or when--some rebel country -wanting to invade our country--we then could call on our allies to chip in –

To help us fight off such an attacker--crude maybe--But in general--that's the way it works--which also means--we may not have always been on the winning team.

I am just "Thought Provoking here — but My logic for expanding on this issue is--because I have not heard of any aboriginal "activists" who have--wanted to join with our Aussies in any of the wars — Yet there have been thousands of individual aboriginals who have Volunteered and joined to help fight-- which is mind boggling really —

In that the aboriginal "activists"- still fought against the British (the Australian Government) at Home--as many thousands of their aboriginal 'brothers and sisters'-- did volunteered and did fight with Australians- to save Australia--**and also to save their Aboriginal Race —** yet the "others" did spend their time — during All those Wars-- trying to make life more difficult for our country and those Living here.?

So often-we read our troops are off somewhere fighting- losing thousands of our young people- trying to build a relationship with say USA--so as when needed — They will jump to our aid as "our allies" — to Help protect our Country. The real worrying part with all that IS--that these "activists" are hiding *in plain view* working toward One Goal

Working to undermine the government--which seems to be how "the elders" were teaching the young aboriginals of today- How-and what to do--still attempting to drive "the invaders"-from their land — as their- Brothers and Sisters-- were IN A War--**Fighting to SAVE Us ALL.!**

Then like for example--my research did find that in fact there were many hundreds of aboriginals' who have volunteered--

To join with Aussies to fight—in each campaign--which was really incredible actually-- when we realise how this on-going campaign of "the elders" Drive The Invaders from Our Land really IS working.!

Naval attacks

Did Germany invade Australia? not actually "invade"-- We had- six German surface raiders operating in Australian waters at different times- between 1940 and 1943.
These ships sank a small number of merchant ships and the Australian light cruiser HMAS Sydney.
The German submarine U-862 also- carried out attacks in our Australian waters in late 1944 and early 1945.

HOW Did We stop the Japanese from invading Australia?
The us naval victory at the battle of midway, in early June 1942, removed Japan's capability to invade Australia by destroying its main Aircraft Carriers.
By the time the last Australian personnel- were withdrawn in 1972, the Vietnam war had become Australia's longest war, eventually being surpassed by Australia's long-term Defence Commitment to the war in Afghanistan.
The Torres Strait is a 150 km strip of crystalline water that separates the Southern coast of new guinea from the tip of Cape York in Queensland.   During the Second world war—

This shallow area of water dotted by Coral cays and islands, proved to be a vital strategic point for the American and Australian forces pushing northwards through new guinea.
By the conclusion of the first 12 months of the Pacific war, 830 Torres Strait island men-- almost every man of eligible age in the area, would volunteer to serve their country.

Thus- was formed *the <u>Torres Strait light</u> <u>infantry battalion</u>*, the only indigenous battalion ever to be formed in our nation's military History-- by July 1942, the Torres strait company was utilised in a counter -attack role, still defending the previous mentioned positions against-- the invasion of the Japanese army on Darwin.!

Darwin--was-- *"an invasion"*--

Planes dropped Bombs-- destroying our Darwin harbour—

Yes--Darwin--
was-*"an Invasion"*!

I ask could anyone in their right mind--not imagine what would have happened--to the aboriginals-
IF-the British so called *"Invaders"* **had not been here in 1942.**
If- "the first fleet" had not built- our government-- built Our population- built weapons- built a defence force-- and had Not Fought IN All of Those Wars--creating "Allies" to help Australia's Defence forces.?
Where all "combined" –
        We defeated the Japanese army.!

So-- TO <u>the aboriginals</u>-- I Say-- **wake up-** --its time- **its time-** to re-think your position---
    it's time to change your *"dream-time stories"*-

It's time to make them become factual and grateful.!

I say- **wake up-** to All <u>governments</u>-

It's time to show some strength--leadership and direction for the indigenous people--time to train them--meld them into Society — Time to teach them **"the real Aussie story"** and way of life--of how true-blue Australians- conduct themselves--

It's time to--propose a History book plan for school children- to include both aboriginal culture and Australian history — To Include 'The Wars'--Highlight what has been built.! Have- some guts--insist on teaching **the real story- and NOT-** a so called indigenous writers made up version showing of our history — showing made up massacres sending-- all the wrong messages--

AND It's time to insert a small indigenous motto/flag right- IN One corner of our National Australian flag —
a representative max. 3.3% of Our Flag Size.

    When combined we are as one nation--

    With the aboriginal flag separate--
        we are still **A Divided** nation.!

    I say--like now--its "time" to wake up--

We need a "multi-cultural" History Story to tell our children.
AND- it's time to compare numbers est. as
Eg:--The British have lost 5,000 in colonisation—
Australia lost 60,000 + 156,000 wounded in- WW1-
Australia lost 34,000 + 31,000 captured in- ww2--
The japanese won "the coral sea" battle-Australia lost-
40,000   in- pacific war--
the Japanese tried to invade australia- where we.
Lost--the Darwin harbour--all bombed/ablaze lost --
11 ships sunk--
lost-- 30 aircraft destroyed-- lost all infrastructure-
Had all defences breached--
Australia lost 3,000 +wounded in- Darwin war--

I point out- that its times like in 1942--when the Japanese landed at Milne bay- **that 'the whole indigenous people'--** *should listen & understand*--**How in Feb.1942--**
The Japanese Bombed- darwin and broome- they--
"massacred"160 'lark force' aussie prisoners.! Our air force held'them back- then they started an invasion via the northern territory- to come overland via the Kokoda trail-- A Combined aussie milita- repelled the Japanese—and then-
We Won—but we lost **72,814 killed + 31,000 wounded** aboriginals incl. --
But then on "the kokoda trail"-our 39th battn. Papua infantry "maroubra force"-helped by 'fuzzy wuzzy's' staged a huge battle--and repelled the Japanese.

Again- I ask "the indigenous" people--
Did your *"dream-time stories"--***tell you** all about this.?
Did they tell you how--to imagine/ **shock horror:--**

What if--the british Had NOT been Here--
"the Japanese-- would have invaded" this land.?
If you had no British/Aussie army — to defend you.? **Question is**--would you--the aboriginal race- have made "friends" with the Japanese-- one of the cruellest army victors known.? .

I SAY:-- You should think about that.?

Of Course--Yes- I know the answer already--
Here now--I have uncovered even more mysteries--with even more questions and more "wondering" — with more of- well- everything.! Yes- my research in this direction has resulted in another world of mystery and intrigue- with more wondering of why the hell would it have happened like that.?

Why- the hell-- wouldn't the Australian population not be told-- made aware of these details.?

The First item being--that I as many Australian's would not have been aware of-- IS-- that each time we sent our Armed forces into one war zone after another--

I now learn that those Armed forces had included hundreds and even thousands of Aboriginals- who had volunteered and who would have been fighting alongside our Aussies. A few-would not have gone overseas-and would have been-- Restricted to help at home as well--and as--their friends in war--the aboriginal race did also lose sons and daughters in their endeavour to help to defend This/Our great nation.

But--why don't the "activists" relate to these things.? Which in itself--poses a surprising revelation to prove that in the main--most of these thousands of aboriginals have seen war--seen and been trained to handle weapons--and from as far back as from world war 1 (ww1) would have learnt how to handle these weapons correctly--how to use them to ward off an enemy--to have seen the destruction from those wars-- they have done this--right through to our latest and biggest saga in defence of Australia--in the Darwin war-- where the Japanese army actually **Did invade-- They did push** into Australia at Darwin--and we fought them off- fighting with allies to fend off the Japanese invasion--as- the Australians armed forces.!

But--what if:--
"the invaders of 1788"-- families-- were not here.? The Japanese army of The 40's- would surely have-
Wiped out--the entire aboriginal race.?
So I Ask:-- did *"dream-time stories"* ever tell you about that.? My guess is — NO-- So I say--
Our governments need to wake up- they-- Need to grow some "Balls"-- they need to--**join all of this Real History in** together- use it- to educate our children in their schools-- not be feeding them with totally bias aboriginal "made up" 'history'" "rubbish" written by some "pretend"or "made up" *would be* aboriginal writers.!

Our history is and should be real — and — Not imagined or **"made-up" Crap.!** **Yes- for all of the years —**

"The activists" have been malaigning aussies-/the government--
I do not understand why "the elders" did not mention anything about **"the battle of darwin"**--
where total casualties were- reported as 72,814. And 31,000 aussies became prisoners-of-war--to die later.
Over 100,000 casualties--
killed by the Japanese; and by august 1945 over a third-- had died in prisoner-of-war camps.

The Aussie armed forces--"the British"--
Have been protecting- saving the aboriginal race--
right from when the Australian combined forces were
fighting in Darwin-- and with some of the aboriginals-- we
had fought and helped to save us all--from the Japanese
Invasion-- yet this is not important enough to rate any
mention by the then prime minister.?
Nor by any of The "activist groups".! --

Darwin--was-- *"a real invasion"*--

I Ask--could anyone in their right mind—
Not imagine—
    what would have happened--
    To the aboriginals-
  IF--"the British"--so called-*"invaders"*--

Had NOT been here-- in 1942.??

Well — now that you all have your eyes Open —
I do herein-- demonstrate Why **aboriginals are not owed anything —** as My Sums on next Page Show--

      Why--**we--should be equal--**
Because —

    we all — have been incredibly — **Conned.!**

So — now I re-iterate--whilst my reader-again will catch--
'a breath'--relax a bit--

To "get over this shock" — here now--

I show you what I am talking about — because when we
      "Compare Losses" —
The deaths as activists *claim* in colonisation — and —
those later-- Killed when fighting to save this country--
including to **save** all the aboriginals--
When we--demonstrate Loss Comparisons--
      The tallies look much as:--

TO-- Re-Iterate-- we-- should be equal.!-

Fact- here recorded.   **Maybe-** no records.
The "invaders"- and--   the "aboriginals"
loss boar war   800
loss ww1   60,000
loss ww2   34,000   loss claimed in settlement
loss pacific   40,000   8,000
                          at end colonisation
                                20,000.?

Loss   darwin   1500   no bodies but--
or — growing--   est. Loss 190,000
est. + **98,000** wounded
large % died later
                          or- say:--235,000 Total..
Est. = 235,000 **plus** wounded--

The tallies say---   we-- should be **Equal**.!
Australa fought in all those wars to help allies who would help us — if we ever had a problem — which we did have a big problem in the 1940's--

So--I say:-- we-- should be equal.!
Because- it was no *"invasion"* of Australia in 1788.
But it was--a real *"invasion"* of Darwin in 1942.

aussiekevG

SUMMARY

IN A Quick Summary — To Look Back--

IT Is hard to Imagine The Natives as Captain Phillips had "Found" on arrival in Botany Bay- then to Learn they were Nomads and Fossickers who wore only Animal Skin loin cloths- and Lived in Humpies as in general- they Hunted Animals for Food and Women who were at most times 'Topless'- with their Full-time occupation as fossicking for Food and teaching their Children how to gather Berries and Fruit and always find water- Both Males- Females and Children learnt Own Language but were all totally--Illiterate as far as a Developed world would be adjudged.

SO often today- We are hearing the Aboriginals- telling us They want to *"Return to Their Culture"*--none of who relate to just *what 'Their Culture' really was Like* — NOR Do they consider that the majority of their Race could Not Survive-- IF they really tried to Live just-- within Their Culture-- Only a few of The Younger Kin of today — could Survive — IF they had to Change to Live as "Their Ancestors" had lived way back in the 1780's--

Today we see 'The Effects' of 200 Years of Constant and continual "Brainwashing" — as most have been gradually Changing — Accepting "The White Mans" education- use of Schooling- their Social and Monetary systems with their Building and always Forward Thinking- ever seeking Asset Growth- A Far cry from The Early Days of the 1780's- where Simple practices of Hunting and Fossicking for Food- was Their Ancestors whole Life- there were none of "The Houses or other Things" of Today — No Ipads- Mobile Phones- no Computers TV or Radio- certainly No Schools and Vehicles Nor Restaurants- Maccas or Pizza or Meat at Supermarkets- Yes- They say they want to *"Return to Their Culture"* — but the "Activists" though- choose Not to Admit that **NO One IS-** Stopping them from 'Going Bush'--doing these things —

But there ARE Three main areas that the whole Aboriginal Race has grown within and around being as:--
IF- Modern Civilisation had Not Found them in 1788. Due to poor Food Supply- lack of Medical services- In Breeding- Then Fighting between 'Tribes' etc-- Their Aboriginal Race surely would have made itself become extinct--
IF- The British- *The First Fleet- had not come- None of their Great Levels of Education- Living Standards- Food- Attire- Transportation-Asset/Wealth- Schooling- could be possible-*
IF- The Descendants of *The British First Fleet- Had NOT been Here to DEFEND The Country and* SAVE *Australia* To **SAVE** *The Whole Aboriginal Race* — **They** *would have been* Wiped Out- *when* The Japanese Army- *Invaded via Darwin* **in 1942.!**
THE AMAZING THING IS — *That the entire Aboriginal Race have refused to Admit or be Thankful for ANY of this- Nor any of what The British have Done for them — How they have HELPED Them — The Aboriginals have refused to Accept that-* **IF They had seriously Wanted to** *"Go Back to Their Culture"-* TO derive NO Physical Help--NO Welfare- and NO Medical Help from The Government — to forsake Home and Assets--**THEY Could have done this**- at any time — But--*IT is Not possible to Have A Cake- and to Eat IT too* — IT must be One Thing — Or-- The Other.!
Which simply means 'The Aboriginals' CAN'T Continue to Accept ALL The Benefits and Welfare given By Government Continue to Enjoy- ALL of The 'Benefits' of Modern Living and **bemoan** that The British Have Taken Their "Culture". AS The Indians say:-- *There- They do talk with Forked Tongue--* THE PROBLEM IS — It is just "The Activists" who make these Claims- **who won't admit that-** First- the majority of Their People just could NOT Survive — in such environment- To Live as Their Ancestors had First Done — OR That They-- Should be Grateful that The Australian Combined Forces--

With Allies FOUGHT The Japanese Army and **SAVED The Whole Aboriginal Race** from being **Wiped Out by Japan.**

HERE as I present on Page 288 herein—whatever Debt 'The Activists' Claimed IS Due to offset Deaths in Colonisation— THESE Debts were Re-Paid IN Full and some in 1942—as The British and Allies **SAVED The Aboriginal Race** from being **Massacred BY The Japan army**—in 1942—Which FAR Outweighed ANY Debts Owed from Colonisation.

YET even today—"The Elders" totally Ignore this FACT— and have continued to Brainwash their People trying to Divide this country-
Their constant Brainwashing has made sure their People--
DO **NOT Admit this FACT**—
Meanwhile-mostly-Top 70% have acquired Top Educations as many have become Professors--are Highly Respected and Smart enough to be In Charge of Universities and Big Businesses—even many Male and Females—have proven to be Experts in various Fields of Sports—and Entertainment— READING THIS—One could say—
Holy Hell—that IS Incredible- was all that really Possible.?
SO—where Do those people who Constantly Complain and frequently Call Out- to be able to **"Return to Our Culture" Come from.?** And—You might well Ask—What IS Wrong with These people—because IF The British had Not come here to Help them—Their whole Race would by now have Deteriorated—OR Wiped Out--YET they will NOT Admit that They Have prospered working with The British.
WHY would they NOT Admit this.? WHY would They Never be Satisfied.? When it is JUST the bottom est. 10% as yet remain living in some types of Humpies today—

YET—to me--IT is amazing that NONE are aware that "Their Elders" have been *"Brainwashing"* them—right from those-- Earlier days—Guiding—Telling them what "The Elders"

Want them to do- Filling their Minds with "Made-Up Stories"-Focused around- *The Massacre at Waterloo Creek* — which-- IS A FURPHY.! **This myth which has ruled The Aboriginal Race for 185 Years — IS Now being Found to be Totally WRONG.!**

BUT Alas — A NEW Myth IS being Created — to again take the place of **The Mythical-- Waterloo Creek** — massacre.! AS In Nov.2023-- A Major Headline says--*The Aboriginals regained A Whole range of Sacred objects — as collected by USA Anthropologist* **Nancy Munn** *as She studied the Warlpiri people from 1956 to 1958. (Story by The Guardian.) A Great recovery for The Aboriginals- as were 350 drawings, 300 photographs and Munn's original journals and notes alongside the sacred objects.* Herein "Hampton Snr"-says- *That collection is now back in Warlpiri hands — getting the Munn objects back is a critical part of teaching the next generation-- and helping them be proud of the heritage and identity by showing what Warlpiri taught linguists, anthropologists- and others-- It's also about truth-telling, about what happened in the Tanami Desert, he says. A lot of our old people, for the first time, were seeing white people-he says 'It's our cultural stuff that was taken'-* **(Very vague) Which was Great- I say — But Now comes** *"The Made Up" 'Story Telling'*--As he says--*Part of that story is about* **the Coniston massacre**- *when Colonisers killed more than 50, and perhaps as many as 200 Warlpiri, Anmatyere and Kaytetye men, women, children in that* **1928** *massacre, which began after a white dingo trapper, Fred Brooks, was found murdered on Coniston station, about 70km from where Yuendemu now is. "we started to bring our younger generation into this community because without them being there, we lose the connection. We have to start collaborating with our young people--* **Telling Stories** *through the objects that we get back, they will get another story, and we pass that information on."* (The Brainwashing Begins) **And here Incredibly--they infer Nancy Munn had written about "The Coniston Massacre".?** But there — I perused much of the Nancy Munn material that she Gathered-and wrote- doing her Research- where I could find NO such mention- as was--

Relating to a *"Coniston Massacre".!* **TO NOTE:--**Here with each Object—Same as *Waterloo Creek* -"The Elders" will now create **"Stories"** to explain what the Object means to them— SO Here come- many more "Made-up" Stories albeit these have NO Connection with Anthropologist Nancy Munn—as she became The Author of **'Walbiri Iconography'** which had **nothing to do with The Claimed-** *"Coniston'* **"Massacre"**— **As Example--**
'An Iconography' is a particular range or system of types of images used by an artist or artists as they convey particular meanings. eg:- in Christian religious painting there is an 'iconography' of images such as a lamb as represents Christ, or the dove- which represents the Holy Spirit.
BUT here again—
Begins another *"Chapter or **Sequence of Made Up-** Stories"* – which the 'Elders' will meld into the constant ***Brainwashing*** AS *Waterloo Creek*--that has been Guiding—and Misleading Young aboriginals since the 1800's—This "Find" has the potential to create another **Giant** *Furphy* as happened with *"Waterloo Creek".!*
As here at Coniston- My Research shows max. 14 Bodies as were found here- Aboriginals say 50 up to 200-- IT will grow and GROW to Boost Numbers as were Massacred"--
BUT Now with The Return of these "Objects"--'The Elders' will Re-Vamp and begin melding these into more of these **"Made-Up Stories"** where-*"The Brainwashing"* **Continues** Just as The esteemed Professor Ryans "Research" continues to GROW as here in Nov.2023 I Found—under Heading:--
How many Aborigines were killed by the British?
The research project, currently in its eighth year- led by University of Newcastle historian Emeritus Professor *Lyndall Ryan, now-- Estimates more than 10,000 Aboriginal and Torres Strait Islander lives were lost in more than 400 massacres, up from a previous--*

Estimate of 8,400 in 302 massacres on 16 Mar 2022 – earlier it was 174 Massacres.? SO – The esteemed Professor Ryan has now 'found'--More Massacre Sites –
But Yet again – She/and The University--HAS Found **NO Bodies** – or NO Body Bones-- to support these Claims – Not at any of these now 400 Massacre Sites – which has taken **Eight Years** of Painstaking Research to Find-- **NO Bodies**-- **I Wonder WHY.?**
Yet- "Bodies" elsewhere keep coming – 230+ Years later--
    HERE I SAY – *Wouldn't IT BE Fantastic* –
    IF *The esteemed- Ms Professor Lyndall Ryan* –
.
*DID Take the Bull by The Horns and DID Lead ALL of Her associates – and Families – to SAY – **Ok Look here** – we have seen enough of this Rubbish – this Made-Up Stuff--*
*FROM Here on – We are going to Focus on **The Darwin War-** Going to LEAD Our People- to **Give Praise to All The Soldiers** including **Our Own Aboriginal People** who DID Join together with Aussies & Allies to **Fight The Japanese Invasion-- at Darwin**--**We don't need to Tell 'Stories' here--** because IT was all TRUE – Imagine what **A Great Effect this will have On our Whole Race.***
Because The Waterloo Creek Massacre- on Jan 26- 1838 –
IS All just an "Elders Long Held MYTH" its "**A Furphy".**
Where The DARWIN War- DID Happen and IF The British HAD NOT Been here The Japanese Army – **WOULD Have Massacred Our Whole Aboriginal Race in 1942--**and for the life of me--I can Not understand WHY- None of The Elders-- Activists-- NEVER Did Mention THIS.? SO-- from here-I Am going to Put this Right for Our Aboriginal Race.!!!
Oh-- I **DO HOPE-- THIS is what** 'Ms Ryan' **really will say.!**
                    aussiekevG.

First- PAUSE, A Moment-- Here IS A List-- of "Kevs" Other Books...
Check with Kev. IF Your Choice IS ready to be released Yet.?

* Kevs What IF Book. **Need Money.?**   ISBN: 978-0-6452499-0-3
* Kevs Wake Up History... "The Aboriginal Furphy". ISBN: 978-0-6452499-7-2

* The 'Cannibal' IS Dead- Hannibal 'Myth'.(Fiction) ISBN: 978-0-6452499-96

* Kevs Neutral Carbon System- Who's To Blame.? ISBN: 978-0-6452499-8-9

* The Bookies Van... Book 1. The Heist.! (Fiction)   ISBN: 978-0-6452499-2-7
                    Book 2. Why IS jack In Prison.? ISBN: 978-0-6452499-3-4

* A Lost Lover...Book 1. Cass " Lost Lover"+ Debie. ISBN: 978-0-6452499-6-5
              Book 2 Cass and 'Dawn'.   (Fiction) ISBN: 978-0-6452499-4-1
.   Book 3. 'Pippa' and Dianne.   ''   ISBN: 978-0-6452499-5-8
              Book 4. 'Joan'   ''
* Kevs "C" Book... (Fiction)   .   ISBN: 978-0-6452499-1-0
            The Book I wrote, when I wasn't writing A Book.!
            A Collection of Short Stories and Antidotes etc

<u>TO COME</u>.
* I Won $$s...Didn't know Of 'Vlahos'- I copped a Backwash
* 'The 'Kaygee' Story...and effect of...'BUT'...
            The Rise and Fall of an un-planned "Empire".
* The Print...The Greatest (Melbourne) Cup Never Run.
* Kevs Horses... A Man and His Farm...Breeding and Racing.!
* Murphys Law... whatever Can Go Wrong...Will Go Wrong.!
            A Collection of 'Murphys' Short Stories.

DO Also Check:--Kevs Seminar Dates & Book Launch Dates on 'Eventbrite'.!

TO ORDER Books:--

Contact Your Bookseller-
   To ORDER "aussiekevG. Books".!

OR—IF any Queries—Contact Kev by--
   Email to:--
   authorkevg@bigpond.com

PS: IF You do Contact Kev--
making Sure to Include YOUR Name—As Reference--
With-- your Contact email etc.

CONTACT Kev.--

   ASK-- IF Your Book Choice IS ready to release Yet.?
   Also Check For:--
   Kevs Seminar Dates OR Book Launch Dates on
            'Eventbrite'.!

DO spare a minute to peruse--
Kevs *"Mind Train"* CARDS
Ref. Page 300
            Kev

Kevs "Mind Train" CARDS

As I Promised — My Readers —
FIRST: So Often — You recall--I said "*To Re-Iterate*" -
as I then Told Parts of This Story —
OVER and OVER — You likely wondered Why.?
Well it was for Several Reasons as:--
To be sure —
    It was to remind you that THIS IS-- What The Aboriginal Life and their actions-- right to Today-- Have Been — and Still ARE-- Based upon —
Repitition — Repitition — Repitition — Repitition--
THEN:--
    IT was meant to TELL My Reader How Very Important These Repetative Things ARE--
AND:--
    IT was also to Advise My Reader — That IF —
You want to USE MY CARDS — To Help You
In what ever IS most Important IN Your Life
Then I needed to Prepare You First —
Because ON The Next Page — What I am about to
Reveal To You — IS **The Most Powerful Positive**
Mental Training and Control Program —
You will ever Find--and--
IF You Chose to Use My Cards — DO **Please** be —
VERY Careful —
    They ARE Just for Personal Use--

DO Please *be Careful* How/where you use Them.!

To Note: — I Do Not Give Advice —
But albeit-- I mould Talk to Friends.

I am NOT A Qualified Practitioner and herein I am
Only Showing My Reader —
What I have Learnt — and What I DO Myself- and--

How I Use — MY **'Mind Trainer CARDS'**.
Because- as Experts say —
  The Mind IS made of TWO Parts--
The Conscious-- which Sees everything —
  Takes IN our Daily Sights and Sounds etc.
The Sub-Conscious--which Stores ALL Information
    we Find- See- and Need to use-for Future-
    And- it Guides and Controls Our Daily
    Thoughts and movements —
    As IT Controls Our Memory.

MY CARDS-Are just A Simple Program — as I use--
TO "Brainwash"- Myself--as Example: —
I Show what I DO — IF You see Value for You —

  Then feel free to follow me and use:--
  KEVS "Mind Trainer" CARDS — (Carefully).

KEVS Mind Trainer CARDS--
I Use Back of 3 Business Cards — Mine currently say-

> **TO My Sub-conscious Mind--**
>
> *I DO NOT Want Covid- thanks.*
>
> *I DO NOT Want **ANY** Other Virisus.*
>
> *I Need to be sure My Balance is Good-*
> *Thank You. .*

So — I Place **ONE Card-** ON The Bedside Table —
I-- Place **ONE Card-** on The Dash of The Car —
I--Place **ONE Card-** on Top Corner of Computer.
TO BE Sure I Do Memorise These Messages-
At First-- I Read The Card — 10 Times — Going to Bed-
I Read The Card-- 10 Times as I Get Up each Morning-
During each Day —
I Physically Look at- and Read The Messages On The Card-
 To TOTALLY Focus on Doing This for 21 Days —
FROM There On- I read it often — Till--
Then-- I need to just Glance AT It — The Sight of The Card--
IS A Reminder to My Sub-Conscious- Tells IT What to DO
AFTER 3 Months — I Could remove The Cards- BUT — I still
prefer to Leave Them there — which helps Me keep MY
Mind Totally Focused ON Those Subjects — This is what I
Call-- MY Personal "Brainwashing" Program.
IF-- I want to Change/ or ADD to The Messages- I Do
Follow the same Procedure- again —
 Please use with Great Caution.!
 Kev

Belatedly — I must advise — ONE Proviso IS Don't take Risks and-- IN Crowds I MUST Remember to Wear My Mask — EG:--I Confess — That having Followed My Cards for 3-4 Years — visiting Supermarkets — Food Venues — Hospitals — We (Wife & I.) both had always Worn Our Masks — and beat COVID — Till attending Our Dear Friends Funeral — back in our Hometown — On the 200klm Drive up — we hit a bad Pothole and Destroyed A Front wheel tyre — So had to Change wheels which badly held us up — Finally arriving at The Funeral Parlor 1 minute before The Service started — Rushing into our Seats — **We forgot to wear Our Masks —** NO Others had Masks on — that didn't faze us before — But here *we forgot*--as we bade Our Dear Friend Goodbye — BUT 3 Days later — I Got Covid — my wife cared for me- till I got better — Next Day — She Got Covid too — so my turn to Care for her — we are now both OK — But it just shows — We broke Our OWN Protocol- **Now we wear Masks again — AND — Study Our Memory CARDS..!**

I EXTEND A BIG **"Thank-You"**-- To My Readers —
I DO Hope You Enjoyed My Story.!
       I Conclude by Saying:--
I DO appreciate You Taking the Time to Read My Book –and--
IF You would like to Pass Your Opinion On It —
Please leave your assessment on The Sellers Site — OR--
I would welcome such by Email to:--
       authorkevg@bigpond.com
       PS:-- **NO Racist Vitriol**-- Please.!
       Kev.

www.ingramcontent.com/pod-product-compliance
Lightning Source LLC
Chambersburg PA
CBHW071955290426
44109CB00018B/2031